GUIDE

TO

LONDON

PANTHEON BOOKS

NEW YORK

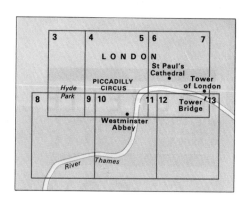

London Regional Transport Underground Map Registered User No. 88/823

ISBN: 0-394-75435-2

ISSN: 0896-0259

Manufactured in the United States of America

First American Edition

4

REGENT'S PARK

St John's Lodge
Bedford College
Open Air Theatre
Queen Mary's Gardens
Inner Circle
York Bridge
Royal College of Physicians

Chester Road
Outer Circle
Inner Circle
Park Square Gardens
Regent's Park
County Court
London Clinic

Varndell St
Robert Street
Clarence Gdns
Longford St
William Road
Church Drummond

National Temperance Hospital
Princeton College

Warren Street
Universi College Hospi

Euston
Warren Street
Royal Orthopaedic Hospital
Cleveland Street

Post Office Tower
Middlesex Hospital Medical School

MARYLEBONE ROAD

York Royal Academy of Music
Madame Tussaud's
Planetarium
Polytechnic of tral London

Marylebone Road
Devonshire Place
Devonshire Street
King Edward VII's Hospital
Weymouth Street
The National Heart Hospital
Fire Station

MARYLEBONE

Portland Place
Carburton Street
Clipstone St College
New Cavendish Street
Foley St
Riding House Street
Middlesex Hospital

New Cavendish Street
Broadcasting House
Polytechnic

Mortimer St
Eastcastle Street
Noel St

Church George Street
Wallace Collection

Queen Anne St
Harley Street
Wimpole St
Wigmore Hall

Cavendish Square
Polytechnic
Gt Portland St
Oxford Circus
Magistrates Court

Wigmore Street
James Street
Duke St

Oxford Street

Oxford Circus

Canopy
Kingly St
Broadwick St

Bond Street
North Row
Audley St
Church

Church Davies Street
New Bond Street

Hanover Square

Conduit Street
Savile Row

WEST E

Brook Street
Grosvenor Square
Roosevelt Memorial
Grosvenor Street

Brook Street

Maddox St
George St
Clifford St
New Bond St

Burlington House (Royal Academy)
Albany

Piccadi
Pic Cir

MAYFAIR

Bourdon St
Bruton Street
Berkeley

Mount Street
Church
Hill Street
South Street

Charles Street
Church Street
Stratton

Piccadilly

Jermyn St
London Library

ST JAM

Curzon Street

St James's

SHEPHERD MARKET

Green Park
Green Park

Pall Mall

Statue of Achilles
Hyde Park Corner
Wellington Museum

Hertford

Piccadilly

St James's Palace
Clarence House

Hyde Park Corner
Wellington Monument

Green Park

Lancaster House

Constitution Hill

Queen Victoria Memorial

St George's Hospital

Grosvenor Cres

Grosvenor Pla

Buckingham Palace Gardens

Buckingham Palace

The Mall

Wellington Barracks

Queen's Gallery

Buckin

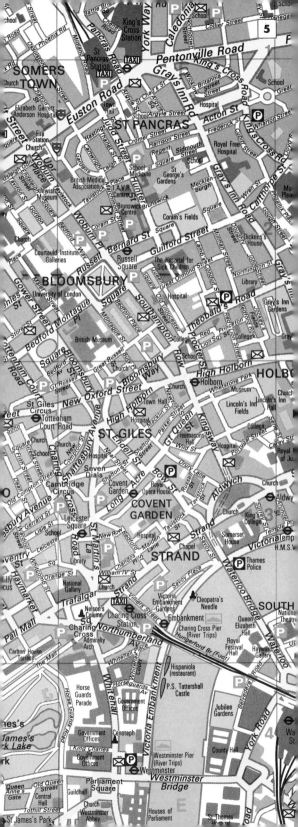

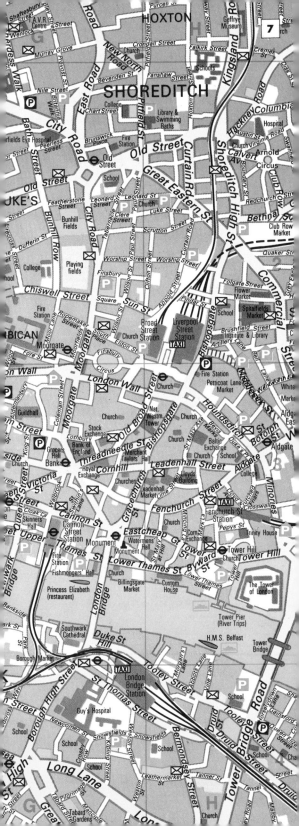

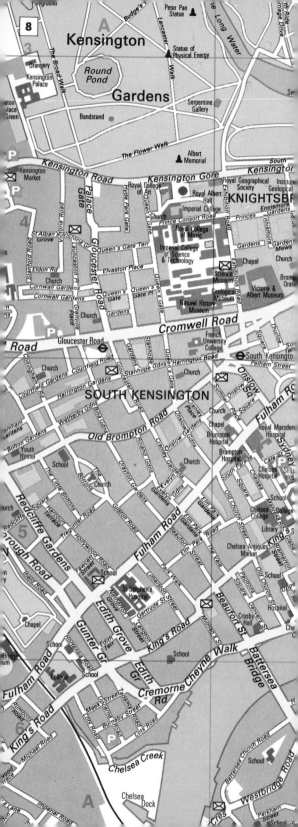

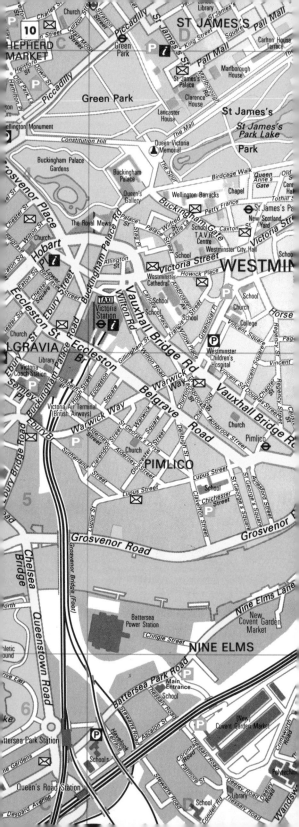

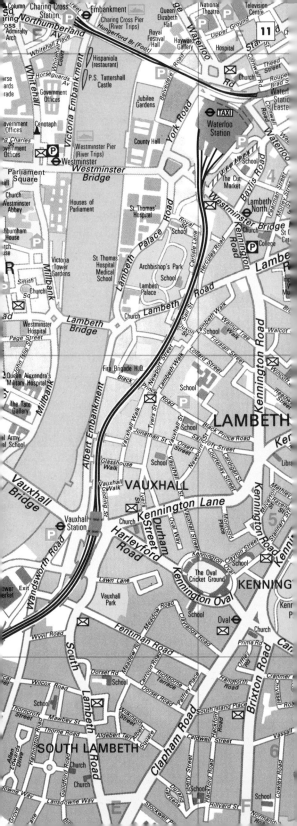

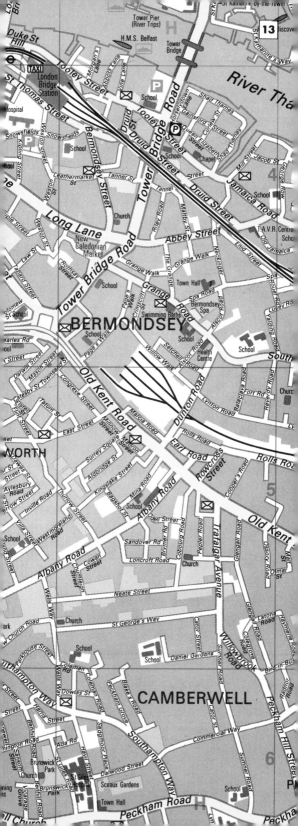

UNDERGROUND

©Copyright London Regional Transport

Daily Services	Peak Hour and Special Services	Daily Services	Peak Hour and Special Services	Daily Services	Peak Hour and Special Services	
Bakerloo Line		Jubilee Line		Piccadilly Line		◯ Interchange with other lines
	peak hours				peak hours	⊛ Interchange with British East
Central Line		Metropolitan Line		Victoria Line		⊡ Interchange with British Rail within walking distance
	peak hours		peak hours			★ Closed Sundays
Circle Line		East London Line		⊛ British Rail		⊞ Closed Saturdays and Sundays
			peak hours and Sunday mornings			▲ Served by Piccadilly Line early mornings and late evenings Mondays to Saturdays and all day Sundays
District Line		Northern Line				† See poster maps at Underground stations for opening and closing times of these stations

London

Eisenbahn / Chemin de fer
Railway / Ferrovia

Einbahnstrasse / Rue à sens unique
One-way street / Via a senso unico

Fussgängerzone / Zone pour piétons
Pedestrian area / Zone pedonale

Öffentliches Gebäude / Bâtiment public
Public building / Edificio pubblico

Park, Sportplatz / Jardin, Terrain de sport
Park, Sportsground / Parco, Campo sportivo

Wald / Forêt
Forest / Foresta

Informationsbüro, Polizei / Syndicat d'Initiative, Police
Tourist information center, Police / Ufficio informazione, Polizi

Parkhaus / Parking couvert
Parking house / Garage pubblico

Theater / Théâtre
Theatre / Teatro

Post, Taxi / Bureau de poste, Taxi
Post office, Taxi / Ufficio postale, Tassi

Schiffsanlegestelle / Embarcadère
Landing place / Debarcadero

Station de métro,
U-Bahn-Station / RER-Station / Station du RER
Underground station. RER station / Stazione di metropolitana,
Stazione di RER

Flughafen / Aéroport
Airport / Aeroporto

Schloss, Kirche / Château, Eglise
Castle, Church / Castello, Chiesa

Denkmal, Ruine / Monument, Ruine
Monument, Ruin / Monumento, Rovina

Campingplatz / Terrain de camping
Camping site / Campeggio

Hallwag

London ●

▶ A century ago, London was the largest city in the world — capital and principal seaport of the first industrial nation and of a world-wide empire. Londoners called it 'The Smoke', a huge conurbation of industry, railways and houses, notorious for its 'peasoup' fogs. New technologies and the passing of time have changed all that. The old industries, the miles of riverside docks, have gone. So too has the empire they served. The City of London remains a world centre of banking and finance, and upholds traditions already old when Dick Whittington was Lord Mayor. Scarlet-coated guardsmen, household cavalry in gleaming breast-plates and plumed helmets, also keep alive the unique pageantry of the London scene. But today's London has, in other ways, changed almost beyond recognition since the days of the Smoke — a process hastened by WWII bombing and post-war reconstruction. The city is a mecca of the arts and entertainment, an arbiter of fashion, once the prerogative of others. Its famous buildings and monuments have been cleaned of centuries of grime. Its many bridges over the Thames, cleaned and re-painted, have a festive look (while salmon once again swim beneath them). And everywhere, new buildings, whole new civic and commercial centres, have transformed the skyline. □

Brief regional history

43-410AD

There is no evidence that there was any permanent settlement on the site of the city of London before the second **Roman invasion of 43AD**. London's real history begins in that year, although there was a Celtic village on the site of Heathrow Airport and evidence of pre-Roman habitations along the Thames at Barnes, Hammersmith, Fulham, Wandsworth, Chelsea and Battersea. The construction of a bridge across the Thames fixed the point from which the Roman city grew, and the bridge was necessary for the Roman legions in their pursuit of the rebellious *Catuvellauni* to their headquarters at Colchester. Once established at the river crossing the settlement quickly became a busy port, trading with continental Europe across the North Sea. A network of roads fanned out from London, the principal ones being Ermine Street (to Lincoln), Stane Street (to Chichester) and Watling Street which, starting at Dover, passed through London on its way north-west to Chester. ● By 60AD, according to Tacitus, London was famous for commerce and crowded with traders. It did not have the status of a *Colonia*, like Lincoln, Gloucester or Colchester, but it was an important commercial centre. ● Although damaged by fire during the Boudiccan Revolt and again in 125AD, the city was substantial by the mid-2ndC with a huge basilica on the site of Leadenhall Market as well as a forum, temples, baths, shops and houses. The military barracks of Cripplegate Fort were built at the north-western edge of the town and by the end of the century a wall of Kentish ragstone had been erected enclosing 325 acres. The four original gates were Aldgate, Bishopsgate, Newgate and Ludgate, whose sites are still crossed by main roads to and from the city. By this time London's population had risen to some 45,000 which it would not achieve again until the 15thC. Remains of the Roman wall can be seen near the Tower of London and the Temple of Mithras is near the Mansion House. There are baths at Cheapside and remains of the forum can be seen near Leadenhall Market. Many Roman artifacts — sculpture, mosaics and metalwork — are now housed in the Museum of London.

410-1065

After the departure of the Romans in 410, London seems to have been abandoned, although it may have provided a temporary haven for Britons retreating before the invaders from the south. Anglo-Saxon farming settlements were plentiful around the original city, which re-emerged into history in 604, when **King Aethelbert** of Kent, having been baptized a Christian by St. Augustine, founded St. Paul's Cathedral and installed Mellitus as bishop there. A subsequent bishop, Eorcenwald, founded the abbeys of Barking and Chertsey; the Church of All Hallows, Barking, dates from about 675. ● In the early 8thC the **Venerable Bede** wrote of London's commercial prosperity, but few details are known of her history until the arrival of the Danes, who raided the city in 839 and returned with a bigger fleet in 851, looting and burning the fragile wooden houses. When **Alfred the Great** made his treaty with Guthrum, London was part of the Anglo-Saxon kingdom of Mercia, the boundary of the Dane-law lying further east. Alfred occupied the city and saw to its defenses before handing it over to Ethelred of Mercia who had married his daughter Ethelfleda. When the Danes came again in 896 the Londoners were able to repel them. ● London did not become the capital city until after the Norman invasion. **Edgar**, the first king of all England, was crowned at Bath, while the West Saxon kings were usually crowned at Winchester. Canute, however, made London his headquarters, holding court on Thorney Island. It was at Thorney Island that **Edward the Confessor** restored the ancient monastery and endowed the famous abbey church of Westminster which was consecrated in 1065, a few days before his death.

1066-12thC

One of **William the Conqueror's** first acts was to confirm the citizens of London in the rights and privileges which they had enjoyed under Edward I. A further tactical move was to place his fortress, the White Tower, just outside the city walls. The **Tower of London** was to remain a symbol of royal might throughout the centuries, acquiring its most sinister reputation under the Tudors. William did not spend much time in London, being much involved with campaigns in England, Scotland and Wales as well as on the continent. The responsibility for commanding a levy of able-bodied men in times of trouble was assigned to Ralph Baynard, who built himself a fortress, Baynard's Castle, on the river at Blackfriars. Another castle, Mountfichet, lay close by. ● Around London were many villages and hamlets mentioned in the Domesday survey, such as Islington and St. Pancras. Marylebone was called Tyburn, after the stream which flowed toward Westminster, forking to make an island where the abbey stood. At Bermondsey, there was a Cluniac priory and another at Kilburn. Among surviving buildings of the Norman period, the Tower, with St. John's Chapel, London's oldest place of worship, stands supreme. ● William Rufus rebuilt the Palace of Westminster, and the great hall which he founded still stands. The chancel of St. Bartholomew's is a relic of the Augustinian priory established under Henry I. Part of the Temple Church, the crypt of St. John's Gate, Clerkenwell and Old St. Pancras Church also date from the 11th and 12thC. William Fitzstephen, writing in 1174, gives a vivid picture of ordinary life in London, with its cock fights, wrestling, javelin throwing and archery contests. There was horse racing at Smithfield and citizens would go hawking in the Chilterns. ● Until 1209 people crossed the Thames by ferry, the Roman bridge having long since vanished. Finally, after many vicissitudes, **London Bridge** was completed with its chapel, shops and buildings and a drawbridge to admit high-masted vessels. Under **Henry I** London received its first **charter**, by which Londoners, independent of any shire, were given direct access to the king. **Guilds** also began at this time, the goldsmiths' and weavers' being the first. These companies also contributed funds directly to the Crown.

13th-15thC

Until the 13thC, government was wherever the king was and the kings and their retinues traveled endlessly. Under **Henry III** London became truly the capital of England and the seat of government. There was the Exchequer with its Chancellor, the Chancery, or legislature, and the Wardrobe with the Privy Seal, which dealt with the king's personal accounts. Henry was also a great benefactor, rebuilding Westminster Abbey and extending the royal palace there. ● Under Henry's son, Edward I, the **Inns of Court** developed. Lincoln's Inn was the first, later to be followed by Gray's Inn and the Temples, which was later divided into the Inner and the Middle Temples. Law was not only administered here but the buildings served as colleges for legal students, there being no university in London. The city and Westminster, originally two separate enclaves, began to be linked as bishops built large houses along the Strand, north of which was the 'convent garden' of the Westminster monks. ● London was the scene of the young King Richard II's confrontation with Wat Tyler and his followers during the dangerous **Peasants' Revolt** of 1381. Tyler's men had crossed the Thames, released prisoners from the Marshalsea and broken into the Tower where they beheaded the Archbishop of Canterbury. Richard's courage in meeting this large army of rebels at Smithfield and listening to their requests was remarkable, and when Tyler was wounded by the mayor, Walworth, the rebels dispersed. Dick Whittington, London's most famous Lord Mayor, served under Richard II, Henry IV and Henry V, becoming very rich with a mansion comparable to a nobleman's house. He gave an immense banquet for Henry V upon his wedding and was among the first to provide conduits of fresh water for the city.

16thC

Around the middle of the 16thC, London experienced a **dramatic growth** of trade and population and between 1530 and 1600 the number of Londoners trebled. With the dissolution of the monasteries, four hospitals were provided to fill their place — St. Bartholomew's, Christ's, Bethlehem (the madhouse known as Bedlam) and Bridewell. Trade was promoted by the establishment of monopolies, such as the Muscovy Company, the Levant Company and the East India Company. The **Royal Exchange** was built in 1566-70 by Sir Thomas Gresham as a meeting place for financiers and merchants. New industries such as silk weaving, glass and pottery making flourished. ● **Henry VIII** began the work of converting York Place into Whitehall Palace and built St. James's Palace across the fields from what is now St. James's Park. Thomas More had a house at Chelsea, where Erasmus was his guest. Noblemen's houses began to appear along the river from Westminster to the city, with gardens down to the water's edge, each with its own watergate. Royal dockyards were built at Deptford and Woolwich. ● The first purpose-built theatre, known simply as 'The Theatre', opened at Shoreditch in 1576. Later the south bank of the river was preferred, although the courtyards of inns, such as that at Southwark, continued to serve as playhouses. Among the new theatres were the 'Rose' particularly associated with Marlowe, the 'Swan' and finally the 'Globe' in which **Shakespeare** had shares and where the plays of Shakespeare, Ben Jonson and Beaumont and Fletcher were performed. Hyde Park became a fashionable venue for the nobility, while Bermondsey was the place where popular festivals and entertainment took place, like bear- and bull-baiting. May Day, a public holiday, saw the erection of Maypoles, particularly that at Leadenhall Street, although these were later banned by the Puritans as pagan emblems. John Stow in his Survey of London of 1598 recalls that all the houses on May Day were 'shadowed in green birch, long fennel, St. John's Wort, white lilies and garlands of flowers'. The Midsummer Watch was another popular festival.

17thC

James I was not inclined to show himself to his people or to go on royal progresses as Elizabeth had. Instead, he preferred to isolate himself in his favourite royal palace of **Whitehall** with his dissolute drinking friends, so that the queen soon set up her own establishment at Denmark House. He planned to extend Whitehall on a grandiose scale, but of the grand scheme only the Banqueting House was completed, designed by Inigo Jones and with a painted ceiling by Rubens. Inigo Jones was also responsible for the Italianate piazza at Covent Garden and for St. Paul's Church there. His masterpiece is the superb Queen's House at Greenwich, begun in 1616, demonstrating his mastery of Palladian Classicism. He also designed masques for royal entertainment with elaborate lighting and scenic effects, often in collaboration with Ben Jonson, as in *The Fortunate Isles* of 1625. ● **Charles I** antagonized Londoners from the very beginning, particularly when Henrietta Maria filled Somerset House with all her French Catholic friends. Always short of money, he made increasing demands upon the city which the city was increasingly reluctant to pay. From 1629 to 1640 he called no Parliament at all. The results were inevitable. The city was staunchly Parliamentarian, raising nine regiments and 16,000 men, when the **First Civil War** broke out. When, after Edgehill in 1642, Charles returned toward a rebellious London, his path was blocked by trained bands at Turnham Green and he promptly retreated. He tried to blockade London by preventing coal from leaving Newcastle, a Royalist stronghold, giving Londoners a bitterly cold winter. He only returned to London in Jan. 1649 for his trial at Westminster Hall. Spending his last night at St. James's Palace, he walked across the park to Inigo Jones's Banqueting House, before which the scaffold had been erected. He died bravely. ● For the next eleven years London was the capital of a Commonwealth and, although the citizens had supported **Cromwell**, they did not find Puritanism, in practice, much to their liking. All the playhouses were closed, music forbidden in church services and choirs disbanded. Furthermore, the city was still constantly being asked for money. It was with jubilation, therefore, that they welcomed the return of the monarchy in the person of **Charles II**. ● In 1664-5 the **plague**, a frequent invader since the Black Death of 1348, killed 75,000 Londoners. The following year the **great fire** burned from 2 to 5 September, consuming four-fifths of the city. St. Paul's, the Royal Exchange, the guildhall and many of the livery halls were gutted, along with eighty-seven parish churches and 13,000 dwellings. Within days **Christopher Wren** had presented a new scheme for the rebuilding of the city and was appointed Surveyor General. Wren designed, or supervised, the rebuilding of fifty-two churches, all but seven of which survive. St. Mary-le-bow in Cheapside and St. Bride's

are famous for their steeples, while many of the interiors, like those of St. Stephen Walbrook and St. Mary
Abchurch are rewarding to visit. Wren's masterpiece,
of course, is St. Paul's Cathedral. He also designed
Greenwich Palace and Chelsea Hospital and provided
additions to the palaces at Kensington and Hampton
Court. The face of London was transformed.

Steeple of St. Bride's, Fleet Street, 1703.

18thC

The 18thC saw the creation of some of London's
most elegant streets and squares. Hanover Square
was built in 1715, Cavendish in 1717, Burlington
House in 1717-20. St. Martin's-in-the-Fields was designed by James Gibbs, and Nicholas Hawksmoor was
responsible for six marvelous churches, like St. Mary
Woolnoth in the city. From the 1770s date Portman
Square, Bedford Square, Portland Place, Somerset
House, the Bank of England, Fitzroy Square and
Baker Street. **Robert Adam** was responsible for many
town houses and for the Adelphi development in the
Strand, the best riverside complex ever seen, now
sadly destroyed. He also worked at Osterley House
and at Syon, transforming old houses and providing
fine Neoclassical interiors. Furniture to adorn the
new houses was made at Chippendale's workshop in
St. Martin's Lane or at Hepplewhite's in Cripplegate.
Paul de Lamerie was making his finest silver, and
John Jackson was printing wallpaper at Battersea.
● In the course of the century merchants, bankers
and landowners grew rich through Britain's burgeon-
ing overseas trade. New bridges spanned the Thames
and cultural life in the capital flourished. This was
the age of Swift, Fielding, Defoe and Sterne, of the
playwrights Goldsmith and Sheridan, of Johnson and

Boswell. Coffee houses were a favourite rendez-vous for writers, politicians and businessmen. Edward Lloyd's was the meeting place of shipping underwriters, for instance. The pleasure gardens of Vauxhall were packed with people and Ranelagh Gardens were opened in 1749, 'the most convenient place for courtships of every kind' wrote Horace Walpole. ● While aristocratic and middle-class life was becoming increasingly refined and elegant, the poor lived in great wretchedness in overcrowded housing with no sanitation. By mid-century, it is estimated that every man, woman and child drank an average of two pints of gin a week — 'Mother Geneva' as it was called. 9,000 children a year died from drink. Crime increased — even the Prince of Wales was robbed in broad daylight in the West End. Hogarth's *Gin Lane* does not exaggerate. In the 1780s, during the **Gordon Riots**, a distillery was sacked and a drunken mob ran amok in the streets for a week before 200 of them were shot dead and order restored. Such were the contrasts of life in a swiftly growing and increasingly self-confident city. ● The **Regency period** could be regarded as a coda to the 18thC, a final flourish of elegance before the dawn of Victorianism. The Prince Regent, later George IV, first employed John Nash to refurbish Carlton House. Later he was to enlarge Buckingham House which became **Buckingham Palace**. But Nash's principal accomplishment was the creation of Regent's Park with its terraces and crescents and the architectural scheme linking Regent's Park to Piccadilly and the Mall to the south. By now, Oxford Street and Fleet Street were lined with elegant shops, lit, after 1812, by gaslight. The streets were full of chaises, carriages and drays in an unending stream. The congested River Thames was provided with docks to make space for the ever-increasing seaborne trade. The West India Dock opened in 1802, the London Dock at Wapping in 1805, the East India a year later. The old coffee houses of the 18thC developed into the gaming houses of the 19thC, like Boodle's and White's. This was the age of the poets Byron, Keats and Shelley and of the painter Thomas Lawrence. Edmund Kean was packing Drury Lane. Sarah Siddons was at Covent Garden. The arbiter of fashion was Beau Brummel.

19thC

Between 1800 and Queen Victoria's death in 1901 the population of London trebled. The rich merchants no longer cared to live in the city of London, and the private houses there were mostly pulled down to make room for ever more warehouses and offices. The age of the commuter had started, to be greatly assisted by the arrival of the **railways** and later of the underground. Many miles of terraced housing were erected for the now clerical class who worked in the city. The numbers of tradesmen, craftsmen, artisans and shopkeepers also increased and, above all, the number of domestic servants. The great buildings of Victorian London were not the town houses but buildings with a much more specific function like the warehouses along the Thames and the great railway terminals like Cubbitt's King's Cross and Brunel's Paddington. ● The new **Houses of Parliament** by Barry and Pugin were completed in 1865, the South Kensington museums were designed in 1851, which was also the date of the Great Exhibition and Paxton's astonishing **Crystal Palace**. Overcrowding and homelessness in

London's East End led to the founding of the Barnardo Homes in 1866 at the same time that William Booth was starting the Salvation Army. Edwin Chadwick, champion of the water closet, was responsible for the Public Health Act of 1848. 1863 saw the arrival of the first **underground** railway and in the 1870s London was criss-crossed with more embankments, bridges and thoroughfares than at any time in her history. The past had to make room for the present.

20thC

Ever more new thoroughfares were built through the centre of London as motorized traffic grew. New hotels, department stores, office blocks and 'mansion' flats were all Edwardian innovations — Harrods was built in 1901-5, Selfridges in 1908, the Ritz Hotel in 1906. **Garden suburbs**, like Hampstead, also date from this time. ● The inter-war years saw the transformation of central London with such buildings as Broadcasting House (1931) and South Africa House (1933). New council estates arose in the suburbs, along with private dwellings in every style from mock-Tudor to mock-Queen Anne. ● The **blitz** destroyed much of London, although St. Paul's miraculously survived, now surrounded with high-rise office buildings like the National Westminster Tower and the high-tech Lloyds Building. The South Bank Arts Complex, begun in 1951 with the Festival Hall, now includes an art gallery, film theatre and the National Theatre. At the **Barbican**, new housing is combined with major cultural facilities. Much has been achieved in the last twenty-five years to preserve the best of London's past and to prevent serious demolitions. The Thames is no longer a sewer as it was in Victorian times but cleaner than it has been for centuries. **Clean Air Acts** have long since banished London's 'peasoup' fogs. The dockland is being intensively developed for residential and office use with widespread restoration of the decaying Victorian warehouses. The city is visited each year by increasing numbers of tourists who can experience nearly 2,000 years of history in the busy streets.

● *Around London*

▶ **BARBICAN***

map 6-G2/Underground: Barbican, Moorgate, St. Paul's.
Bus: 5, 55, 4, 63.

The 60-acre site, named after a medieval watchtower, corresponds to the area of London most devastated during WWII. Plans were drawn up soon after for its redevelopment as a combined commercial, residential and recreation centre, but this most ambitious of all post-war London development was only finished in 1981. The most striking feature is the 412-ft. tower blocks, part of the housing scheme.

City livery companies

As early as the 1stC AD, a Roman historian described the City of London as a 'busy emporium for trade'. The City, the oldest part of the capital, with its own government (the Corporation) and its own Lord Mayor, has remained busy — though its importance now resides in the fact that it is an international centre for banking, insurance and stockbrokering. Although its buildings were largely destroyed by the great fire of 1666, a number of its institutions and traditions date from medieval times. Many of these are connected with its guilds or livery companies.

Guilds were the first workers' organizations in England, and were formed to protect the interests of people practicing a certain trade or craft, and to monitor the way they carried out their business. By the 13th and 14thC, they had become very powerful, and in London were known as livery companies because of the particular dress or 'livery' they wore. The companies also became wealthy enough to finance charities, schools and almshouses for their members as well as churches. In outdoor performances of mystery plays each guild would stage a biblical scene appropriate to its trade — the fishmongers for example, would perform Jonah and the Whale.

There are now ninety-six companies, each with various officials and about 20,000 members. These include the mercers, grocers, drapers, skinners, apothecaries, saddlers and many more. Although membership is now largely an honorary matter, the guilds often give aid to the trades with which they are connected by name and take part in activities related to their trades. For example, the goldsmiths' company is responsible for stamping hallmarks on gold and silver articles. In addition to the main guildhall (the seat of the City of London's government for a thousand years), various livery companies have their own magnificent halls. These may be viewed by the public on certain days, and the companies hold annual banquets there. On these occasions a loving cup of hot mulled wine or of punch is passed from guest to guest: while each person drinks, the men on either side of him stand up until he has finished — this dates from the time when a man holding the cup would be unable to reach for his sword and defend himself if attacked, so his neighbours would act as bodyguards. Each year the livery companies elect a Lord Mayor of London. The new Lord Mayor stages a pageant (the Lord Mayor's Show) on the second Saturday in November. The following Monday there is a lavish banquet at the guildhall, usually attended by the Prime Minister.

▶ The **Arts and Conference Centre** (N side), includes a concert hall, exhibition gallery, library, cinema and theatre (London home of the Royal Shakespeare Company). ▶ Next to it is the Guildhall School of Music and Drama; founded in 1880, the school moved into its new premises in 1977. ▶ **London wall** marks the S limit of the site, with sections of the original Roman wall. ▶ At the W end is the **Museum of London** (*Tue.-Sat., 10-6; Sun., 2-6*), presenting aspects of the city's life from prehistoric times to the present; also houses the Lord Mayor's coach (1757), which takes to the streets once a year in the Lord Mayor's Show. ▶ The 16thC church of **St. Giles Cripplegate** is also within the Barbican complex; John Milton is buried in the churchyard. □

▶ BATTERSEA*

map p. 96-B1/British Rail: Battersea Park.

For most people, Battersea, facing Chelsea (→), Victoria and Pimlico (→), on the bank of the Thames, means a famous power station, a maze of railway lines around Clapham Junction and grimy Victorian streets. For centuries Battersea was renowned for its market gardens and such local industries as pottery and copperware. The coming of the railways turned it into an industrial suburb. Now its character is changing again.

▶ **Battersea Park**, right by the river, was opened in 1853. It was given a big face-lift for the 1951 Festival of Britain, with a new pleasure garden and works by sculptors Henry Moore and Barbara Hepworth. It is now a popular South London venue for fairs and carnivals. ▶ A short walk W of the park is **Old Battersea House**, a fine late 17thC manor house. ▶ E of park is the monumental **power station**, designed by Sir Giles Gilbert Scott. Built in the 1930s, it no longer functions, but plans are afoot to turn it into a leisure centre. ▶ Close by is the famous Dogs' Home, a canine orphanage. ▶ Further still is the **New Covent Garden** fruit and vegetable market.   □

▶ BETHNAL GREEN AND SHOREDITCH

map p. 96-B1/Underground: Bethnal Green, Old Street.

Bethnal Green was the poorest district of Victorian London, noted for its Labour Yard, where men broke stones for a bowl of soup. This century's slum clearance and a falling population have changed the area. Neighbouring Shoreditch has theatrical connections. England's first playhouse was erected here in 1576, before being moved and re-erected as the Globe Theatre in Southwark (→). Richard Burbage, actor and friend of Shakespeare, also lived here.

▶ **Bethnal Green Museum of Childhood** (Cambridge Heath Road, E2) has dolls, dolls' houses, puppets and toy theatres *(Mon.-Thu., Sat., 10-6, Sun., 2.30-6)*. ▶ The **Geffrye Museum** (Kingsland Road): former almshouses; displays of English furniture and furnishings from Tudor times onwards, also a reconstructed Georgian street *(Tue.-Sat., 10-5, Sun., 2-5)*. ▶ To the S is **Spitalfields**, East London's fruit, vegetable and flower market. ▶ Facing it is **Christ Church** (Hawksmoor), now being restored *(not regularly open to the public)*.   □

▶ BLACKHEATH*

map p. 96-B2/British Rail: Blackheath.

The heath, above Greenwich (→) and the Thames, stands on the historic approach to the capital from Dover and the continent. Henry V was welcomed there after Agincourt, as was Charles II upon his Restoration. The rebel armies of Wat Tyler and Jack Cade gathered there before marching on London. In the 17th and 18thC, the Dover Road made it a notorious place for highwaymen. Residential development in the late 18th and 19thC gives the area its elegant character.

▶ **Colonnade House** and the crescent-shaped **Paragon** (1790) are fine examples of late Georgian domestic building. ▶ Just E of the heath, **Morden College** (1695), attributed to Wren; chapel carvings probably by Grinling Gibbons; large and handsome almshouse group in its own grounds, still a home for the elderly *(visits by appointment only)*.

Nearby

▶ **Charlton House** (Charlton Road) London's best- preserved Jacobean building (*Mon.-Fri., 9-5, wkend by appointment*). ▶ **Eltham Palace** (off Court Yard, Eltham); 15thC great hall with fine hammer-beam roof (*Apr.-Oct., 10.30-12.15, 2.15-6, Thu., Sun.; Nov.-Mar.: closes at 4*). ▶ **Severndroog House** (Shooter's Hill), 18thC Gothic folly; local landmark on site of earlier beacon (*not open*). □

▶ BLOOMSBURY*

map 5-E3/Underground: Russell Square, Tottenham Court Road, Euston Square, Goodge Street. Bus: 14, 19, 22, 24, 29, 30, 73.

In the Domesday Book, Bloomsbury was noted for its vineyards. Its real development began in the late 17thC with the creation of Southampton (later Bloomsbury) Square — the first London square so named. Through the 18th and early 19thC, its Georgian and Regency squares made it London's most fashionable area. Early this century it attracted writers and artists who formed the 'Bloomsbury Group'. Today it is the home of London University and related institutions, the British Museum (→) and many publishing houses.

▶ Its garden squares — many named after former estates — include **Bedford** (the best preserved), **Bloomsbury** itself, **Fitzroy** (with work by Robert Adam), **Gordon**, **Russell**, **Tavistock**, **Torrington** and **Woburn**. ▶ Near the British Museum (→) is **St. George's Church** (1716), designed by Nicholas Hawksmoor with imposing Classical portico and unusual tower, in the form of a stepped pyramid, crowned by a statue of George I posing as St. George. ▶ In complete contrast is **Congress House** (1958), TUC headquarters, with sculpture by Epstein. ▶ **Senate House** (1932), headquarters of London University, for many years the capital's tallest building. ▶ The **Courtauld Institute Galleries** (Woburn Square) has Renaissance, Impressionist and post-Impressionist paintings including Degas, Manet, Gauguin, Van Gogh, Cezanne (*Mon.-Sat., 10-5, Sun., 2-5*). ▶ The **Percival David Foundation** (Gordon Square) has Chinese ceramics of eight countries (*Mon., 2-5; Tue.-Fri., 10.30-5; Sat., 10.30-1; Cl. Bank Hols.*). ▶ **Pollock's Toy Museum** (Scala Street): mainly Victorian toy theatres, dolls and dolls' houses (*Mon.-Sat., 10-5*). ▶ **Telecom Tower** (1963), formerly Post Office Tower, London's tallest structure (580 ft.) until the 1981 **NatWest Tower** in the City (→). ▶ **University College** (1827), with Classical portico and dome by William Wilkins, architect of the National Gallery (→). ▶ The **Jewish Museum** (Upper Woburn Place; *May-Sep.: Tue.-Fri., 10-4, Sun., 10-12.45; Oct.-Apr.: Tue.-Thu., 10-4,Fri., Sun., 10-12.45*): ritual objects and antiquities of Jewish life and worship. □

▶ BRITISH MUSEUM***

map 5-E2/Gt. Russel Street. Underground: Tottenham Court Road. Bus: 14, 19, 22, 68, 73, 77A, 188.

One of the world's greatest collections of historical treasures, founded 1753. The main part of the present building, with massive south-facing Classical portico and colonnade, was constructed between 1823 and 1847, to designs by Sir Robert Smirke. Later additions include the circular, copper-domed Reading Room (1857) by Sydney Smirke; Edward VII Galleries (1914) and Duveen Gallery (1938). Major bequests include George IV's library of 65,000 volumes and Lord Elgin's Parthenon sculptures.

▶ **Parthenon sculptures** (Elgin Marbles, room 8); **Palace of Nineveh sculptures** (room 21); **Rosetta Stone** and Egyptian monumental sculptures (room 25); ▶ British Library exhibits, including **Magna Carta, Lindisfarne Gospels, Shakespeare First Folio, Gutenberg Bible** (rooms 29-33); Oriental ceramics and sculptures (room 34); **Mildenhall treasures** (room 40); **Sutton Hoo Anglo-Saxon burial ship and treasures** (room 41); **Isle of Lewis chessmen** (room 42); ▶ Clocks and watches (room 44); ▶ Coins and medals (room 50); ▶ Egyptian mummies, tomb paintings, papyri (rooms 60-66) (*Mon.-Sat., 10-5, Sun., 2.30-6; Cl. Bank Hols.*). ☐

▶ BUCKINGHAM PALACE*

map 10-D4/Underground: Victoria, St. James's Park. Bus: 11, 24, 29.

Official London residence of the reigning monarch, the palace takes its name from Buckingham House (1715). Bought by George III in 1762, Nash converted it into a royal residence (1820). Much enlarged by Edward Blore (1830-47) for Queen Victoria and her family, there were further renovations and additions by Sir James Pennethorne (1853) and by Sir Aston Webb, who added the East front (facing the Mall →) in 1913. The present building has some 600 rooms, and there is a large garden, with lake, at the back. The royal standard flies over the palace when the monarch is in residence.

▶ The **Queen's Gallery** (Buckingham Palace Road) once the palace chapel, has changing exhibitions from the royal collection of paintings and drawings (*Tue.-Sat., 11-5, Sun., 2-5; Cl. Mon. ex. Bank Hols.*). ▶ The **Royal Mews** (Buckingham Palace Road) by Nash, and separate from the palace, houses the various royal coaches, including the Gold State Coach (1762) used at coronations (*Wed. Thu., 2-4; Cl. Ascot week and during state visits*). ▶ The **Changing of the Guard**, the ceremony performed at 11.30 in the palace forecourt by detachments of the Brigade of Guards, daily in summer and alternate days in winter. ☐

▶ CEMETERIES*

The city's dead were for a long time buried in the churchyards of local parish churches, but by the 17thC these were overcrowded and a danger to health. New burial grounds were then established near the city limits. These, in turn, were filled, and, during the 19thC many, like Bunhill Fields (→Clerkenwell and Finsbury), were turned into public gardens. At the same time, large new cemeteries were opened on the perimeter of the rapidly growing suburbs. Most of these remain, containing monuments to many famous people and offering remarkable examples of mainly Victorian funeral architecture and imagery.

▶ **Highgate** (1839), best known of London's cemeteries, situated on a slope of the hill, and centered round an Egyptian-style necropolis or circle of catacombs. The old part, with the graves of Michael Faraday, George Eliot, Dante Gabriel Rossetti and John Galsworthy, is being restored after long neglect and vandalism; the new part has the grave and striking monument to Karl Marx. ▶ **Kensal Rise** (1833), with Greek Revival chapel, catacombs and the graves of I.K. Brunel, Leigh Hunt, Thackeray and Trollope; adjoining, Roman Catholic cemetery, with the graves of Francis Thompson and conductor Sir John Barbirolli. ▶ **Brompton** (1840), with large octagonal, domed chapel, Classical Revival catacombs and the graves of George Borrow and suffragette Emmeline Pankhurst. ▶ **City of London Cemetery** (1856), largest municipal cemetery in

Europe, well landscaped and maintained, with imposing monuments to those transferred there from City churchyards. ▶ An unusual addition to London's burial grounds and cemeteries is the **Pets' Cemetery**, on the N side of Kensington Gardens (→), with monuments to pet dogs, cats, monkeys and birds.   □

The great fire of London

One of the city's tallest buildings is the Monument (202 ft.) which was erected in 1677 to commemorate the great fire which caused havoc eleven years before. Only six people died in the blaze, but the old medieval city was burned to the ground over an area of about 400 acres, 80,000 people (more than half of the population) were left homeless and eighty-seven churches and 13,000 houses were destroyed.

The fire started in the house of the royal baker in Pudding Lane very early on Sunday morning on 2 Sep. 1666. There was a strong wind blowing from the east, and the fire burned without stopping until 6 Sep. It spread so quickly and seemed to blaze up in places so far away from the main fire, that many thought it had been started deliberately by Dutch or French enemies or papists (Catholics). The great 17thC diarist Samuel Pepys gave a graphic account of the fire (as he did of the great plague which had swept the capital the previous year) and recorded how he buried his gold and silver valuables in his father-in-law's garden for safekeeping.

Although it caused destruction on a massive scale, the fire was not without its beneficial effects. The architect Christopher Wren drew up a reconstruction plan for the whole of London and, although it was not implemented, Wren was given the job of redesigning St. Paul's Cathedral, which had been destroyed. Wren also designed more than fifty other churches besides, as well as many important public buildings including the Monument, Greenwich Observatory, the Royal Exchange and Chelsea Hospital.

The great cathedral is acknowledged to be his masterpiece, and Wren's tomb bears the inscription: 'Reader, if you would seek his monuments, look around you'.

▶ CHELSEA*

map 9-B5/Underground: Sloane Square. Bus: 11, 14, 19, 22.

In 1520, Sir Thomas More built a country house in the area, followed by Henry VIII. The Porcelain Works of 1745 (closed fifty years later) gave Chelsea an even wider fame. Neat 18th and 19thC streets and squares, the home of many celebrities, plus antique shops and fashion boutiques give Chelsea its charm and chic.

▶ **Cheyne Walk** has 17th, 18th and 19thC houses and gardens facing the Thames. ▶ Standing back from the river is **Chelsea Old Church** (All Saints), with Norman origins; inside are monuments to Sir Thomas More and others, and the only chained books in a London church. ▶ **Carlyle's House** (*Wed.-Sun., Bank Hol. Mon., 11-5*), a Queen Anne house largely preserved as the writer knew it. ▶ By **Chelsea Embankment** is the **Physic Garden** (1676), one of the oldest botanical institutions. ▶ The **Royal Hospital**, founded by Charles II for veteran soldiers (Chelsea Pensioners) and built by Wren (1682); visit the **chapel** and **great hall** (*Mon.-Sat., 10-12, 2-4, Sun., 2-4*) and adjacent **museum** (*Mon.-Fri., 10-12, 2-5, Sat., Sun., 2-4.30*) devoted to the hospital's history; mementoes of

Wellington. ▶ **Ranelagh Gardens** are the scene of the Chelsea Flower Show (*May*). ▶ Close by is the **National Army Museum** (*Mon.-Sat., 10-5.30; Sun., 2-5.30; Cl. Bank Hols.*): British Army relics of five centuries. ▶ **Kings Road.**, named after the path taken by Charles II to Nell Gwynne's house in Fulham, has stylish antique shops, boutiques, restaurants and pubs. ▶ **Sloane Square** has the **Royal Court Theatre** and Peter Jones, the architecturally praised 1936 department store. ▶ In Sloane Street is **Holy Trinity** (1888), rich in pre-Raphaelite decoration, with windows by Burne-Jones.   □

▶ CHISWICK*

map p. 96-A1/Underground: Turnham Green, Chiswick Park. British Rail; Chiswick, Kew Bridge.

On a bend of the river W of Hammersmith (→), Chiswick remained almost a village until a little over a century ago, when a shipyard and other local industries, plus the railway, brought a rapid rise in population. Many old houses remain and the district has pleasant parks and riverside walks.

▶ **Chiswick Mall** on the river front preserves the village atmosphere with 17th, 18th and 19thC houses. ▶ Round the corner is **St. Nicholas Parish Church** (origins 12thC), where William Hogarth is buried. ▶ Nearby is **Hogarth House** (*Apr.-Sep.: Mon, Wed.-Sat., 11-6, Sun., 2-6; Oct.-Mar.: Mon., Wed.-Sat., 11-4, Sun., 2-4*) with drawings, engravings and other relics of the artist. ▶ Well away from the traffic is **Chiswick House** (Burlington Lane; *mid-Mar. - mid-Oct.: 9.30-6.30; mid-Oct.-mid-Mar.: Wed.-Sun., 9.30-4*), designed as a residence for and by Lord Burlington (1725) in the Classical Revival (Palladian) style, with fine interior decoration by William Kent, who also landscaped the grounds.

Nearby

▶ The **Musical Museum** (High Street, Brentford), a unique collection of mechanical pianos, organs and other instruments, also phonographs and musical boxes (*Mon.-Sat., 10-5, Sun., 2.30-6; Cl. Bank Hols.*). ▶ **Kew Bridge Engines Trust** (Kew Bridge Road, Brentford; *Sat., Sun., Bank Hol. Mon., 11-5*): a museum of early steam engines (sometimes working), traction engines and models.   □

▶ CHURCHES**

Underground: Chancery Lane, Blackfriars, Barbican, St. Pauls, Mansion House, Bank, Monument, Liverpool Street, Aldgate, Tower Hill. Bus: 6, 9, 11, 15, 22, 25.

Before the Great Fire of 1666 there were 87 City churches. The fire destroyed or badly damaged 76 of them. Fifty-one were rebuilt, many by Wren. Some had gone again by WWII. The war took a further toll. But over thirty remain (some much restored), 23 by Wren.

▶ **St. Andrew Holborn** (Wren), with the tomb of Thomas Coram (→ Holborn and St. Pancras). ▶ **City Temple** (1874). ▶ **St. Bride** has Wren's tallest steeple (226 ft.); WWII bombing revealed Roman remains in the crypt, now a museum. ▶ **St. Dunstan**, Fleet Street. ▶ **St. Benet** (Wren), where Inigo Jones is buried. ▶ **St. Andrew-by-the-Wardrobe** (Wren). ▶ **St. Bartholomew the Great** (1120), London's oldest church, with Norman nave. ▶ **St. Giles Cripplegate** (→ Barbican). ▶ **St. Sepulchre**, a 12thC crusader's church, connected with old Newgate Prison and with music. ▶ **St. Vedast** (Wren): ▶ **St. Martin Ludgate** (Wren). ▶ **St. Mary-le-Bow** (Wren). WWII destroyed the famous bells, but tower and steeple, Wren's finest, survive. Norman crypt. ▶ **St. Michael Paternoster** (Wren): burial place of Richard Whittington, commemorated in stained glass. ▶ **St. Nicholas Cole Abbey** (Wren). ▶ **St. James Carlickhythe** (Wren). ▶ **St. Mary Aldermary** (Wren). ▶ **St. Stephen Walbrook** (Wren) interior, with dome, anticipates features of St. Paul's; Sir John Vanbrugh's burial place. ▶ **St. Lawrence Jewry** (Wren). ▶ **St. Mary Woolnoth** (Hawksmoor). ▶ **St. Margaret Lothbury** (Wren). ▶ **St. Michael Cornhill** (Wren, Hawksmoor). ▶ **St. Peter-upon-Cornhill** (Wren). ▶ **St. Edmund the King** (Wren). ▶ **St. Mary Abchurch** (Wren): painted dome and reredos by Grinling Gibbons. ▶ **St. Magnus the Martyr** (Wren): Miles Coverdale buried in the tiny churchyard, with relics of Roman wharf and old London Bridge. ▶ **St. Margaret Pattens** (Wren). ▶ **St. Helen Bishopsgate** (14thC): fine monuments, brasses and a memorial window to Shakespeare. ▶ **All Hallows London Wall** (G. Dance). ▶ **St. Botolph Without Bishopsgate** (G. Dance). ▶ **St. Katherine Cree** (17thC): ceiling with livery company coats-of-arms. ▶ **St. Andrew Undershaft** (16thC). ▶ **St. Botolph Aldgate** (G. Dance). ▶ **All Hallows-by-the-Tower** (8th, 17th, 20thC), with fine brasses. ▶ **St. Olave** (15thC). □

▶ **CITY**

map 6-G3/Underground: Blackfriars, St. Paul's, Bank, Monument, Tower Hill. Bus: 6, 9, 15. British Rail: Blackfriars, Cannon Street, Fenchurch Street, Liverpool Street.

The City of London is the oldest part of the capital, with its own form of government and institutions. The first real chapter of its history is that of Roman township, *Londinium* (A.D. 50-400), of which fragments of wall and foundations of various buildings survive. William I (1066) and King John (1215) both granted the City charters giving it a large degree of autonomy. Loans to Edward III and Henry V to fight foreign wars increased its political power and independence. It also grew rich through trade and banking, aided by links with the German Hanseatic League, Italian Lombards, Flemish weavers, French Huguenots. The medieval City spread beyond the Roman walls to occupy an area almost exactly one square mile, and that has remained its limit. Its resident population fell dramatically as the rest of London grew, but it remains a world financial centre and thrives on its traditions.

▶ **Temple Bar**, marking the site of the old gateway, marks the City's limit. South of it is **The Temple** (→). ▶ **Fleet Street** is the home of many national newspapers — note the *Daily Express* building (1932) in Art Deco style. There is also **Prince Henry's Room** (no. 17, *Mon.-Fri., 1.45-5, Sat., 1.45-4.30; Cl. Sun., Bank Hols.*) with Tudor and Jacobean decoration; **Dr. Johnson's House** (*May-Sep.: daily, 11-5.30. Oct.-Apr.: Mon.-Sat., 11-5; Cl. Bank Hols.*), where he compiled his Dictionary; **St. Bride Printing Library** (Bride Lane) with early presses and type displays (*Mon.-Fri., 9.30-5.30*). ▶ Along **Newgate** is the **Central Criminal Court** (*Old Bailey*), with the well-known gilt statue of Justice atop the dome, on the site of old Newgate Prison. ▶ The **National Postal Museum** (*Mon.-Fri., 10-4.30, Sat., 10-4; Cl. Bank Hols.*); mainly 19thC British stamps. Close by is statue to Sir Rowland Hill, founder of the penny post. N of St. Paul's Cathedral (→) is the Barbican (→). ▶ **Bank of England** (The Old Lady of Threadneedle Street), centre of the nation's finances. The earlier building, by Sir John Soane, was largely rebuilt (1921-37). ▶ **Royal Exchange** (1841; *Mon.-Fri., 10-4, Sat., 10-12; Cl. Bank Hols.*), formerly the Stock Exchange; frequent exhibitions. A carillon plays at certain times. ▶ **Mansion House** (1739), official residence of the Lord Mayor. On the front pediment is an allegory of London defeating Envy with Plenty, Father Thames looking on. ▶ The present **Stock Exchange** (1973), Threadneedle Street, has a public gallery and cinema (*Mon.-Fri., 10-3.15; Cl. Bank Hols.*). ▶ **Lloyd's of London**, in its striking new building (1986) by Leadenhall Market, houses the *Lutine Bell*, tra-

Maundy money and hot cross buns

The word 'maundy' comes from the Latin mandatum meaning 'command', and it is associated with the command Jesus gave his disciples as he symbolically washed their feet before the Last Supper. The command was that they should love one another.

From the time of Edward III in the 14thC, it was the custom for the King of England to wash the feet of poor people in remembrance of that command. Every Maundy Thursday (the day before Good Friday), the feet of London poor people would be cleaned in warm scented water by the Yeomen of the Laundry; the king would then carry out a ceremonial washing and clothing would be distributed. Ever since 1689 the giving of money has become known as Maundy Money. Each person receives specially minted silver pennies equal in value to the age of the king or queen. The money is contained in small leather purses which are distributed by a Yeoman of the Guard. Bunches of sweet-scented flowers and herbs are carried, and the clergy carry linen towels over their shoulders as a reminder of the washing ceremony that used to take place. Since 1953, the ceremony, which used to be held at Westminster Abbey, takes place in cathedrals around the country.

On Good Friday, it is still the custom all over England to eat hot cross buns. Similar buns flavoured with spices and currants or raisins were enjoyed in the 16thC during the period of Lent. At this time all loaves of bread and buns were marked with a cross to ward off evil spirits before being put in the oven. After the Reformation this practice was stopped for all baking except that of the buns eaten on Good Friday, the day commemorating the Crucifixion.

ditionally struck for the loss or safe arrival of a ship. ▶ Another new building is the nearby 600-ft. **NatWest Tower** (1981), Britain's tallest. ▶ N of the Bank is the **Guildhall** (→). ▶ Wren's Monument (1671; *May-Sep., 9-5.40, Sun., 2-5.40; Oct.-Apr., 9-3.40; Cl. some Bank Hols.*); a 202-ft. column with viewing platform, commemorating the Great Fire (1666). ▶ By London Bridge (→) is **Fishmonger's Hall** (1841); imposing city livery company building. ▶ Nearby are the old buildings of **Billingsgate** fish market (1875) and the **Custom House** (1817). ▶ **Trinity Square Gardens**, facing the **Tower of London** (→), includes a section of Roman wall. ▶ Behind is **Trinity House** (1794), which administers the nation's lighthouses. ▶ E is the old **Royal Mint** (1809), just outside the City limits. □

▶ CLERKENWELL AND FINSBURY*

map 6-F2/Underground: Barbican, Faringdon, Old Street, Angel. Bus: 6, 9, 11, 15, 19.

Just N of the City (→), on rising ground, watered by springs and Fleet Riber, Clerkenwell (Clerk's Well) and neighbouring Finsbury long enjoyed a favoured situation. After the Great Fire (1666), population overspill brought in clockmakers and other craftsmen, while local spas remained popular. The 19thC was a time of slums and industrial unrest — a focal point for the Chartists. Slum clearance and rehousing have transformed the scene, but much Georgian architecture remains.

▶ **Charterhouse Square**, mostly Georgian, with adjacent remains of Charterhouse itself (*Apr.-Jul: Wed., 2.45*): 14thC priory, then a famous school (now moved from London). ▶ By **Smithfield Market** and Square (just within the City), **Cloth Fair**, site of the old Street Bartholomew Fair, with 17thC houses. Next to it the church of **St. bartholomew the Great** (→Churches). ▶ **St. John's Gate** (off Clerkenwell Road), 16thC gateway to 12thC priory, now a museum (*Tue., Fri., Sat., 10-6*) with relics of the Crusaders' order that founded the priory. ▶ **Clerkenwell Green** has the Karl Marx Memorial Library, where Lenin worked. ▶ **John Wesley's House and Chapel** (*check on opening times*) now a museum for the founder of Methodism who is buried in the chapel yard. ▶ **Bunhill** (Bone Hill) **Fields**, with tombs of Bunyan, Blake, George Fox. ▶ **Eagle pub**, inspiration of a popular old song, has many music-hall prints. ▶ **Sadler's Wells Theatre** (1931), on the site of a spa, pleasure garden and earlier theatre, one-time home of a famous ballet and opera company, now changed into the Royal Ballet (Covent Garden) and English National Opera (Coliseum). □

▶ COVENT GARDEN**

map 5-E3/Underground: Covent Garden. Bus: 6, 9, 11, 15.

Covent (Convent) Garden, on the fringes of Westminster (→), was quite rural until the mid-17thC, when Inigo Jones built his large Italian-style piazza of town houses and church that has largely shaped the area's character and appearance ever since. The 18thC craze for coffee houses and the proximity of two great theatres attracted Garrick, Goldsmith, Sheridan and Pope. Taverns, gaming houses and brothels also gave the area a bad name. The famous vegetable, fruit and flower market, dating from the 17thC, soon grew too big and was never properly managed; it moved to Battersea (→) in 1974.

▶ The Victorian Market Hall in the centre of the cobbled piazza is now an arcade with shops and cafes, plus street entertainers. ▶ On the piazza's W side is **St. Paul's Cathedral**, which Inigo Jones called 'the handsomest barn in England', famous as the setting for the opening of Shaw's *Pygmalion* and the musical *My Fair Lady*. Samuel Butler and Thomas Arne, composer of 'Rule, Britannia', are buried there. ▶ The Flower Market building, on the SE corner, is now the **London Transport Museum** (*daily, 10-6*), housing some of the capital's old buses, trams and trains. ▶ The **Theatre Royal**, Drury Lane (1810), fourth theatre on the site, is one of London's largest and most handsome; it is supposed to be haunted. ▶ The **Royal Opera House** (1857) is also on the site of earlier theatres. Many great singers — Caruso, Melba, Gigli, Tauber, Flagstad — have appeared there. ▶ Facing it is Bow Street police station, reminder of the Bow Street Runners of 1753. ▶ **Lamb and Flag** pub (Rose Street, 1623) is where the poet John Dryden was attacked by footpads. □

▶ DULWICH*

map p. 96-B2/British Rail: West Dulwich, North Dulwich, Forest Hill, Crystal Palace.

This fashionable South London district, once a hunting ground for English kings, remained a village and small spa (Dulwich Wells) until the 19thC. It has, to a large measure, kept its rural character, with 18th and 19thC cottages around the road named Dulwich Village and the only toll gate still operating in the London area.

▶ Standing in its own grounds off College Road is **Dulwich College**, an imposing group of buildings in Victorian Renaissance style. It was founded in 1619, by

Edward Alleyn, impresario and acquaintance of Shakes-peare. ▶ Connected with it is the **Picture Gallery** (Sir John Soane, 1814; *check on opening times*), England's oldest public art gallery, with works by Raphael, Rembrandt, Rubens, Van Dyck, Canaletto, Gainsborough, Reynolds. ▶ **Kingswood House**, now a community centre and library, is a local landmark in 19thC Gothic style.

Nearby

▶ The **Horniman Museum**, built in Art Nouveau style, hous-es a collection of tribal masks, musical instruments and other artifacts gathered by its founder, F.J. Horniman, during his travels as a tea merchant. ▶ **Crystal Palace Park**, Sydenham, named after Joseph Paxton's Crystal Palace Exhibition Hall, moved here from Hyde Park (→) after the Great Exhibition of 1851 and burnt down in 1936. Surviving is a group of model prehistoric monsters grou-ped round the lake. Today the park is a major sports centre.   □

▶ **EALING***

map p. 96-A1/Underground: Ealing Broadway, Acton Town. British Rail: Ealing Broadway.

Up to the beginning of the 19thC, Ealing was still a rural retreat for the landed gentry. By the end of the century, it prided itself on being 'The Queen of the Suburbs', on account of its good housing, public ame-nities and transport — qualities still possessed by this large residential W London district.

▶ **Pitshanger Manor**, Walpole Park, converted 1800, by Sir John Soane from an existing manor house. Long used as borough offices, there are plans to open it to the public. ▶ **St. Benedict's** bright Neogothic church (1897) is on the site of a much earlier Benedictine abbey. ▶ **Gun-nersbury Park** and **Estate** has an interesting history, including ownership by the Rothschild family. It has a 19thC Gothic folly, orangery and two Regency houses, the larger of which, **Gunnersbury House**, is a museum of local history (*Mar.-Oct.: Mon.-Fri., 9-5, Sat., Sun., Bank Hols., 2-6; Nov.-Feb.: Mon.-Fri., 9-4, Sat., Sun., Bank Hols., 2-4*).   □

▶ **GREENWICH***

map p. 96-B1/British Rail: Greenwich, Maze Hill.

Four miles downstream from Tower Bridge (→) and rising above a broad bend of the river, Greenwich has some of London's finest sights and places of interest. The 15thC Greenwich Palace was a favourite with Tudor royalty, especially with Henry VIII, who was born there. After the Restoration, Charles II put in hard work on the great series of buildings for which Greenwich is now famous. By the 18thC it was also a thriving township — well placed between the Dept-ford and Woolwich shipyards — attested by the many Queen Anne and Georgian houses that still grace its streets.

▶ **The Royal Naval College**, completed 1726 and formerly the Royal Naval Hospital (*daily ex. Thu., 2.30-5*) stands on the site of the old palace. Mainly the work of Wren, Hawksmoor and Vanbrugh, the whole is best seen from the river. ▶ The magnificent **Painted Hall** is the work of James Thornhill and the place of Nelson's lying-in-state. ▶ Facing it, Wren's chapel, gutted by fire 1779, restor-ed in Neoclassical style. ▶ The two wings of the Natio-nal Maritime Museum (*Easter-Oct.: Mon.-Sat., 10-6, Sun., 2-5.30; Nov.-Easter: Mon.-Fri., 10-5, Sat., 10-5.30, Sun., 2-5*) commemorate the Battle of Trafalgar and house a great collection of globes, maps, charts and navigational instruments, model ships and barges, uniforms (including Nelson's), guns and other equipment; also paintings by Canaletto, Hogarth and Reynolds. ▶ Between them, and linked by colonnades, is the **Queen's House** (1635), designed in the Italian Palladian style by Inigo Jones and a part of the museum. ▶ The **Old Royal Observatory** (*Easter-Oct.: Mon.-Sat., 10-6, Sun., 2-5.30; Nov.-Mar.: Mon.-Fri., 10-5, Sat., 10-5.30, Sun., 2-5; Cl. Bank Hols.*) atop the hill of **Greenwich Park**, dates from John Flamsteed's 1675 appointment as the first Astronomer Royal. Flamsteed's House (Wren) and the later Meridian and S buildings (with Planetarium) house telescopes, sun dials, clocks and other astronomical relics. The famous brass meridian line divides the E and W hemispheres. There is also a statue to General Wolfe, a citizen of Greenwich. ▶ On the waterfront, next to the college, are two famous ships: the clipper, *Cutty Sark* (1869), converted into a museum (*Nov.-Mar.: Mon.-Sat., 10.30-5, Sun., 2.30-5; Apr.-Oct.: Mon.-Sat., 10.30-6, Sun., 2.30-6*) and Sir Francis Chichester's yacht *Gipsy Moth IV* (1966). ▶ **Croom's Hill**, running up the E side of the park, has several notable 17th and 18thC houses. ▶ Below it is **St. Alfege**, rebuilt 1718 by Hawksmoor. The composer Thomas Tallis and General Wolfe are buried here. ▶ Above, on the edge of Blackheath (→), with fine **views** over London, is the 18thC **Ranger's House** (*daily, 10-5 ex. Good Fri., Christmas*) displaying Jacobean and Stuart portraits. ▶ West of the park is **Vanbrugh Castle** (1726), a fanciful dwelling the architect and playwright built for himself. ▶ The **Trafalgar Tavern**, **Yacht Tavern** and **Cutty Sark Tavern** all have views of the river. □

▶ GUILDHALL*

map 7-B3/ off Gresham Street. Underground: Bank. Bus: 6, 9, 11, 22, 25.

The guildhall is the centre London's civic life. Lord Mayors have been elected there since 1192. It has also seen some famous trials, including that of Archbishop Cranmer (1553). The 15thC building was mostly destroyed by the Great Fire (1666) and rebuilt. It was wrecked again in WWII and later restored. Parts of the 15thC structure, including the crypt, survive.

▶ The **main hall** (*daily, 10-5; Sun. in May-Sep., 2-5; Cl. Bank Hols.*), where the annual Lord Mayor's Banquet is held, contains the coats-of-arms and banners of the twelve great city livery companies, statues to Nelson, Wellington , Churchill and replicas of the large wooden figures of Gog and Magog, mythical founders of pre-Roman London. ▶ The **library** (*Mon.-Sat., 9.30-5; Cl. Bank Hols. and for official functions*), first endowed by Richard Whittington, 1423, has manuscripts, maps and prints relating to the history of the City and of London as a whole. ▶ The **Clock Museum** (*Mon.-Fri., 9.30-5*), the collection of the Worshipful Company of Clockmakers, has over 700 exhibits covering five centuries of horology. □

▶ HAMMERSMITH AND FULHAM*

map p. 96-A1/Underground: Hammersmith. Bus: 9, 11, 73. Underground: Putney Bridge. Bus: 14, 22, 30.

Hammersmith has long been a busy place, with coaching inns astride the main road from London to the West. Its high population and continued position as a vital traffic junction have today made it busier than ever; though only a few minutes' walk from the Broadway and the Flyover, the river front is a haven of calm. The life of neighbouring Fulham once centred round the Palace of the Bishops of London, then grew rapidly as a large Victorian suburb.

▶ Lower Mall and Upper Mall follow the river from Hammersmith Bridge (→Thames Bridges) to Chiswick (→), with 18th and early 19thC houses, once inhabited by such celebrities as artist William Morris. ▶ **St. Paul's Church** by the Broadway dates from 1882, but has interior decoration taken from an earlier church by Wren, and a fine monument to Charles II. ▶ **Fulham Palace**, a 16thC Tudor manor house, was the official residence of the Bishops of London until 1973. Adjoining **Bishops' Park** borders the river and looks across to boating yards on the Putney bank. ▶ Nearby **All Saints Church** was largely rebuilt in the 19thC, but is rich in monuments and brasses, including two from the time of the Civil War; fourteen Bishops of London are buried in the churchyard. ▶ **Fulham Pottery** is commemorated by a 'bottle kiln' preserved on the original site.   □

▶ **HAMPSTEAD AND HIGHGATE***

map p. 96-B1/Underground: Hampstead. Bus: 24. Underground: Archway. Bus: 19.

Hampstead, climbing steeply towards the heath, was a popular 18thC spa, and with its period houses and

---

London's underground

Despite its name, much of the underground system — certainly when it reaches the outer suburbs — runs above the ground. The first underground, the Metropolitan Railway, was actually little different from the railway in that it used ordinary steam trains. These ran on lines constructed in shallow trenches and then simply roofed over — the so-called 'cut-and-cover' method of construction. Nevertheless, at the time it opened, the Metropolitan provided a revolutionary kind of urban transport. On its first day, in 1863, the line carried 30,000 passengers, and extended from Paddington Station in the west to Farringdon Street in the city. With the addition of the District Line, this was to develop into the inner circle. Other lines were built by different companies, and in 1890 the first 'tube' was introduced by the City and South London Railway (later the Northern Line). This was made by boring through the earth underground, and necessitated elevators to take passengers down to the deeper levels. Electrification further transformed the system, which has continued to develop throughout the present century. In 1933, the whole group of underground railways was united with the bus company to form the London Passenger Transport Board. As the lines extended further into the rural areas surrounding London during the inter-war years, the suburbs developed. During WWII many stations provided shelter against the bombing raids — beds were ranged in rows along the platforms. 20thC improvements to passenger comfort have included sprung upholstered seats, escalators, automatic doors and turnstiles. Recent additions to the service are the Victoria and Jubilee lines and the Piccadilly Line extension which gives travelers the opportunity of going directly from central London to Heathrow Airport.

pleasant location has long been North London's most fashionable district, the home of many famous people. Highgate, on the far side of the heath, has retained a little more of its own village atmosphere than bustling Hampstead.

▶ **Hampstead Heath**, London's highest point, with **views** right across the capital; long a refuge at times of crisis — the Black Death, the Plague and the Great Fire. It now attracts large crowds to its Bank Holiday fairs. ▶ Two famous pubs on the heath are **Jack Straw's Castle**, named after a leader of the Peasants' Revolt of 1381, and **The Spaniards Inn and Toll House**, used by the famous highwayman Dick Turpin. ▶ Also on the heath is **Kenwood House** (*Apr.-Sep.: daily, 10-7; Oct., Feb. and Mar.: 10-5; Nov.-Jan.: 10-4*), very fine 18thC mansion, largely the work of Robert Adam, with beautiful interiors and paintings by Rembrandt, Frans Hals, Vermeer, Gainsborough, Romney; summer open-air concerts are given in the grounds. ▶ Just below the heath is **Keats House** (*Mon.-Sat., 10-1 and 2-6, Sun., 2-5*), a Regency dwelling with relics of the poet and his contemporaries. ▶ **Church Walk** is a Georgian enclave, with St. John's parish church of the same period; the artist John Constable is buried there. ▶ Nearby is **Fenton House** (1693) (*Apr.-Oct.: Mon.-Wed., Sat. and Sun., 11-6*), a notable museum of keyboard instruments and porcelain; and **Romney's House** (1797) with distinctive weatherboarding. ▶ Highgate's **Waterlow Park** includes 16th-18thC **Lauderdale House**, home of Nell Gwynne. Next to it is **Highgate Cemetery** (→ Cemeteries).

Nearby

▶ **Alexandra Palace** (Muswell Hill) was built in 1875 to rival the Crystal Palace (→ Dulwich). The world's first television transmission was made from it in 1936; now an exhibition hall. □

▶ HAMPTON COURT**

map p. 96-A2/British Rail: Hampton Court.

Hampton Court Palace (*Apr.-Sep.: Mon.-Sat., 9.30-6,Sun., 11-6; Oct.-Mar.: Mon.-Sat., 9.30-5, Sun., 2-5*) was the home of English monarchs from Henry VIII to George II. Begun by Cardinal Wolsey, 1515, it was already the grandest Tudor palace in England when Henry acquired it in 1529 and enlarged it further. In 1689, at the behest of William and Mary, Wren demolished part of it and, working with Grinling Gibbons and others, added a big new wing. Thus the present building, as well as housing many historical and art treasures, is a remarkable marriage of the Tudor and English Renaissance styles.

▶ The **great hall**, one of the finest examples of Tudor construction, is also the oldest surviving English theatre, used by Elizabeth I; 16thC Flemish tapestries. ▶ The **Great Watching Chamber** has a paneled and decorated ceiling and more Flemish tapestries. ▶ The **Cartoon Gallery** was specially designed by Wren and Gibbons to display cartoons by Raphael. ▶ Throughout the apartments there are also paintings by Mantegna, Titian, Giorgione, Veronese, Correggio, Holbein, Van Dyck. ▶ The **Astronomical Clock** (1540) shows the hour, month, date, signs of the zodiac, year and phase of the moon. ▶ The **gardens** include the Broad Walk, surveying the Great Fountain Garden and Long Water; the Great Vine, planted by the landscape artist Capability Brown (1768); the Wilderness and **Maze**. ▶ **Hampton Court Green**, facing the palace, has period houses, including the Old Court House, Wren's home (1706-23). ▶ Nearby **Bushy Park**, formerly a royal hunting reserve, has an avenue of chestnut trees and the Diana fountain, laid out by Wren. □

▶ HOLBORN AND ST. PANCRAS*

map 5-E2/Underground: Holborn, Chancery Lane. Bus:
22, 25, 68, 77A, 188. Underground: Kings Cross. Bus: 14,
30, 73, 77A.

Holborn (Holebourne, a tributary of the Fleet River),
on the edge of the City, grew rapidly in the 17th and
18thC, as a centre of the legal profession and the diamond and silver trades. The area of St. Pancras, further N, was still rural until the coming of the railways,
when St. Pancras and Kings Cross stations
(→Railway Stations) changed it into an industrial quarter.

▶ **Lincoln's Inn Fields**, one of London's largest squares,
has **Sir John Soane's Museum** (*Tue.-Sat., 10-5; Cl. Sun.,
Bank Hols.*), the architect's home, exactly as he left it,
with models and drawings of his work and that of Robert
Adam; drawings and etchings by Piranesi, paintings by
Hogarth, Canaletto, Reynolds, Turner, and, at the rear
(the Crypt), his collection of Egyptian, Greek and Roman
antiquities. ▶ Across the square is the **Old Curiosity Shop**
(1567), after Dickens' novel of the same name (but not the
actual one), selling gifts and curios. ▶ **Lincoln's Inn**, in its
own grounds, is one of the legal Inns of Court, with the
old hall (1492), the **gatehouse** (1518) and **chapel** (1619;
restricted opening hours). ▶ Chancery Lane has the
Public Records Office Museum (*Mon.-Fri., 1-4*) with a
copy of the Domesday Book and many letters and documents dating back to the 14thC; also the London Silver
Vaults (*Mon.-Fri., 9-5.30, Sat., 9-12.30*). ▶ **Staple Inn** with
its **hall** (1580) is fronted on High Holborn by timbered
houses (1586) that recall London before the Great Fire.
▶ The Victorian **Holborn Viaduct** (just in the City) crosses
Farringdon Street, the old course of the Fleet River.
▶ **Hatton Garden**, a street, is London's diamond and
jewelry centre. There is also an old charity school (1696)
with the figures of two children; in adjoining Ely Place,
St. Ethelreda's Church with crypt (1251) and fragments
of Roman wall. In the connecting passageway is **Ye Olde
Mitre** pub (1546). ▶ **Gray's Inn**, another of the Inns of
Court, has the **gatehouse** (1688), rebuilt **hall** with Tudor
paneling said to come from the wood of a Spanish gal-
leon, and a statue to Sir Francis Bacon, patron of the Inn,
who laid out the gardens. ▶ **Bedford Row** and **Doughty
Street** are fine Georgian terraces, the latter with **Dickens'
House** (*Mon.-Sat., 10-5; Cl. Bank Hols.*), with mementos
of the novelist. ▶ **Coram Fields**, now a children's park,
the site of the Foundling Hospital, established by Thomas
Coram (1742). The **Thomas Coram Foundation** (*Mon.-Fri.,
10-4; Cl. for conferences*) includes items from the hospital's patrons, paintings by Hogarth, a fair copy of Handel's
Messiah and other scores. ▶ **St. Pancras New Church**
(1822), modeled on the Erechtheion and other antique
Athenian landmarks. ▶ **St. Pancras Old Church** has
Saxon origins and Norman features; Sir John Soane is
buried here, in his own mausoleum.   [ ]

▶ HOUSES OF PARLIAMENT*

map 11-E4/Underground: Westminster. Bus: 3, 11, 12, 24,
29, 53, 88.

Officially the Palace of Westminster, there being a
palace on the site since the time of Edward the Confessor (1042-66). Almost from the start, it was also a
place for debate (a parliament) and legislation, by
stages becoming the main seat of government, and the
scene of such dramatic events as the Gunpowder
Plot (1605) and Charles I's demand for five members
of the House of Commons (1642), the prelude to Civil
War. In 1834 fire destroyed most of the area, and the
present Gothic Revival building (1837-60), with 1000
rooms and two miles of corridors, rose in its place

Cockneys

Strictly speaking, the only true cockneys are those Londoners who are born within the sound of Bow Bells. In days gone by, the street traders and other working people in the East End evolved a language of their own which made them unintelligible to outsiders. This 'rhyming slang' as it is known, was developed, it is said, to confuse the police who were always ready to pounce on the market trades for obstruction and other forms of public nuisance. Two or three words would be substituted for the word intended — the only connection being that they rhymed. Thus 'apples and pears' stood for 'stairs', 'Hampstead Heath' for 'teeth' and 'bacon and eggs' for 'legs'. To make matters more confusing, only the first word of the phrase would be used in conversation: so if a man commented on a girl's lovely bacons, he would be referring to her legs, and if he said he'd lost his uncle he would really mean he couldn't find his shirt (from 'Uncle Bert'). 'Hat' was abbreviated to 'titfer' (from 'tit for tat'). While the East End community is not as tightly knit as it was 100 years ago and rhyming slang is no longer quite the private code it once was, many of the words and phrases have been more universally adopted. Many Londoners and others, for example, frequently say that somebody talkative 'rabbits on' without realizing that they are actually using the short form of 'rabbit and pork'.

Cockney traders had their own ceremonial dress too. This was quite unlike everyday market wear and consisted of suits of clothes each decorated with thousands of mother-of-pearl buttons, sewn overlapping each other to make patterns. With these costumes the men would wear silk mufflers and the women, enormous ostrich feather hats. Those entitled to sport such finery were called pearly kings and queens and were elected by the different boroughs from among the important members of the street trading community. In the past, these 'kings' and 'queens' did charity work for the old and poor in their areas, and once a year would attend a special harvest festival service in the Old Kent Road. Although the service still takes place (now in St. Martin's-in-the-Fields), there are few 'pearlies' left. However, the Pearly King of the city of London still attends Petticoat Lane market every Sunday.

to designs by Sir Charles Barry and Augustus Welby Pugin. It was damaged in WWII and restored by Sir Giles Gilbert Scott.

▶ The two main external features, best seen from Westminster Bridge or from across the river, are the **Victoria Tower** and the **Clock Tower**, known as **Big Ben** after the bell that strikes every hour. ▶ In **Old Palace Yard** is a statue of Richard I (the Lionheart); facing the Victoria Tower is the **Jewel Tower**, a part of the old palace, and beyond, the **Victoria Tower Gardens**, with a cast of Rodin's *Burghers of Calais* inspired by an event in Anglo-French history. ▶ **Westminster Hall**, with its massive hammer-beam roof (1400) is the major surviving part of the old palace. It has seen royal banquets, the trials of Sir Thomas More, Anne Boleyn, Guy Fawkes and Charles I, the proclamation of Oliver Cromwell as Lord Protector (his statue stands outside), and, in more recent times, the lying-in-state of Sir Winston Churchill. ▶ **St. Stephen's Hall** connects it to the Central Lobby, thence to the House of Commons, with the Speaker's Chair, the Table of the House on which stands the mace. ▶ The **Royal Entrance**, beneath the Victoria Tower, leads to the most richly decorated apartments: the Robing Room, Royal Gallery and the **House of Lords** with the Throne for State Openings of Parliament and the woolsack for the Lord Chancellor (*access to House of Commons debates by queuing or application to your M.P.; tours of Westminster Hall by application to M.P.*).   [ ]

▶ HYDE PARK**

map 3-B3/Underground: Hyde Park Corner, Marble Arch. Bus: 9, 12, 14, 15, 19, 22, 30, 52, 73, 74, 88.

Bordered by Park Lane, Knightsbridge and Bayswater Road, and merging to the W with Kensington Gardens, Hyde Park was first opened to the public in 1637, when it was still on the outskirts of the capital. It has served as military camp and arsenal, duelling ground and haunt of footpads, fashionable carriage and riding venue, and in 1851 as the site of the Great Exhibition (the Crystal Palace). In 1961 it lost some of its land to the widening of Park Lane, but remains London's most accessible and popular open space.

▶ **Hyde Park Corner**, the junction of Park Lane, Knightsbridge and Piccadilly, has WWI memorials to the Royal Artillery and Machine Gun Corps; a statue to the Duke of Wellington; and Decimus Burton's Greek-Corinthian Constitution Arch (1827), crowned by the bronze chariot of Victory, and Greek-Ionic Scree, both originally planned as a royal link between Buckingham Palace (→) and the park.
▶ **Apsley House** (Robert Adam, 1771-1829; *Tue.-Thu., Sat., 10-6, Sun., 2-6; Cl. Bank Hols.*), Wellington's home contains household and military effects, paintings by Correggio, Vermeer, Brueghel, Rubens, Velazquez, Goya; also mementoes of Napoleon. ▶ Facing Apsley House from the park is the **Achilles** statue (1822), cast in bronze from captured French guns, another tribute to Wellington.
▶ **Rotten Row** (*route du roi*) is an equestrian way. William III had lamps hung from the trees — the first English roadway to be lit. ▶ The **Serpentine**, now a boating lake and swimming pool, was created 1730 by damming the Westbourne River. Nearby is the old Powder Magazine (1805). ▶ **Speaker's Corner**, at the junction of Park Lane, Bayswater Road and Oxford Street, designated a place of public debate 1872, is famous for its orators. Across the roadway is Marble Arch (1827), Nash's entrance to Buckingham Palace, moved to its present site 1851.   [ ]

▶ IMPERIAL WAR MUSEUM*

map 12-F4/Underground: Lambeth North, Elephant Castle. Bus: 1, 3, 12, 53, 63, 68, 159, 171, 188.

Founded in 1917 and devoted mainly to British Empire and Commonwealth involvement in the two World Wars, the museum is housed in what was part of the Bethlehem Royal Hospital for the Insane (Bedlam). The dome and portico were added in 1838 by Sydney Smirke, architect of the British Museum Reading Room.

▶ WWI Mark V tank, **Sopwith Camel** combat aircraft, 'Ole Bill' London bus troop carrier. ▶ WWII RAF **Spitfire** fighter aircraft, RAF Lancaster bomber fuselage, Italian manned torpedo, German V flying bomb. ▶ **Drawings and paintings** by British war artists: Henry Moore, Paul Nash, John Piper, Laura Knight, Augustus John; in addition, frequent special exhibitions and film shows. The museum also maintains the Cabinet War Rooms (→Whitehall) and *HMS Belfast* (→Thames; *Mon.-Sat., 10-5.30, Sun., 2-5.30*).
    [ ]

▶ **KENSINGTON****

map 8-A4/Underground: Lancaster Gate, High Street Kensington, South Kensington.

Part of the district, on rising ground above the old Thames flood plain, attracted the aristocracy from the 17thC on, their dwellings — Campden House, Holland House, Gore House — remembered in local place names. William and Mary's move to Kensington Palace enhanced its reputation still more. Prosperous urban growth in the 19thC, plus great public buildings and institutions, has maintained Kensington's prestige.

▶ **Kensington Gardens** are a continuation of Hyde Park (→), with the Fountain Garden, Queen Anne's Alcove (Wren), Peter Pan's statue and G.F. Watt's *Physical Energy*. Nearby is the 18thC Round Pond. ▶ Still in Kensington Gardens, the **Serpentine Art Gallery**, once a tea-house, has frequent exhibitions. ▶ The Gothic-Revival **Albert Memorial** (1872) to Queen Victoria's husband Prince Albert, designed by Sir George Gilbert Scott, has figurative ornamental stonework. ▶ Facing it across Kensington Gore is Francis Fowke's massive **Royal Albert Hall** (1870), decorated outside by a frieze around the dome, *The Triumph of Art and Letters*. Inside is seating for 8,000 and a 150-ton organ, the world's largest when installed; home of the famous summer Promenade Concerts. ▶ Grouped around the Albert Hall are the Royal Colleges of Art, of Organists and of Music, and the Imperial College of Science with Italianate tower and dome. ▶ **Kensington Palace** (1690; *Mon.-Sat., 9-5, Sun., 1-5*), on the W edge of the gardens, is part Jacobean but mainly the work of Wren and Hawksmoor, commissioned by William III. Queen Victoria was born there. The King's Staircase has murals by William Kent, and the Gallery paintings by Rubens and Van Dyck; 17th and 18thC furnishings, personal mementoes of Queen Victoria and a collection of court dresses. By the Broad Walk is the Sunken Garden and Orangery. ▶ Just off Kensington High Street is **Kensington Square**, one of the oldest and best preserved, with plaques to famous inhabitants. ▶ Further down the High Street are the **Commonwealth Institute** (1962; *Mon.-Sat., 10-5.30, Sun., 2-5*) with exhibits from 40 Commonwealth countries, plus film, theatre and dance shows; **Leighton House** (1866; *Mon.-Sat., 11-5; Cl. Bank Hols.*), home of the Victorian painter Lord Leighton, with a mosaic Arab Hall and 19thC paintings. ▶ Behind is **Holland Park** and **House** (1606), Jacobean in origin, but bombed in WWII and much restored; setting for open-air plays and concerts. ▶ Situated close together are the **Natural History** (→), **Science** (→) and **Victoria and Albert** (→) Museums; plus the **Geological Museum** (*Mon.-Sat., 10-6, Sun., 2.30-6*), with displays of fossils, gemstones and a piece of the moon. ▶ On Queen's Gate is **Baden Powell House** (*daily 8-10.30 p.m.*) with a memorial exhibition to the founder of the Scout Association.

▶ **KEW GARDENS****

map p. 96-A1-2/Underground: Kew Gardens. British Rail: Kew Bridge.

The Royal Botanical Gardens, Kew (*winter 10-4 daily, summer 10-8*) grew in size and splendour under royal patronage from the 17thC onward. In 1772 they were landscaped by Lancelot Capability Brown; in 1841, the 300-acre gardens, with over 20,000 species of plant, were given to the nation, both as a park and as a scientific institution.

▶ **Kew Palace**, also known as the Dutch House, a Jacobean mansion by the river, has a 17thC herbal garden. ▶ Other monuments to royal patronage include the **Orangery**, three 18thC Greek-style temples, the **Pagoda**, the

Queen's Cottage, a thatched summerhouse and **King William's Temple**. ▶ The two largest conservatories, both
designed by Decimus Burton and the engineer Richard
Turner, are the **Palm House** (1844), the finest iron and
glass structure of its day, and the **Temperate House**
(1860). ▶ The General Museum faces the Palm House
across the pond. ▶ The **Japanese Gate** commemorates
an exhibition. ▶ The **Marianne North Gallery** has a collection of over 800 botanical paintings by the artist. ▶ Close
by is the 225-ft. flagstaff, made from the trunk of a Dou-
glas fir, presented by the government of British Columbia. ▶ **Kew Green**, by the main entrance to the gardens,
is graced by Georgian and Regency houses. The interior
of St. Anne's (1710-70), like the gardens, has benefitted
from royal patronage; Thomas Gainsborough is buried
there.   [ ]

▶ KNIGHTSBRIDGE AND BELGRAVIA*

map 8-B4/Underground: Hyde Park Corner, Victoria,
Knightsbridge.

Knightsbridge takes its name from an old bridge over
the River Westbourne (→Hyde Park, the Serpentine),
where two legendary knights met in combat. Through
the 17th and 18thC, both it and adjoining Belgravia
were neglected in favour of Kensington (→) to the W.
But in the 19thC they grew rapidly, becoming one of
London's most exclusive areas, with embassies, institutions, famous shops and department stores.

▶ Facing Hyde Park Corner (→Hyde Park) is the Classical-Revival building of **St. George's Hospital** (1827).
▶ Behind it is elegant **Wilton Crescent**; also **Belgrave
Square** (1825-40), one of London's grandest, planned by
Thomas Cubitt and George Bavesi in Regency style. A
recent addition is a statue to Simon Bolivar. ▶ Neighbouring **Eaton Square** (1826-53), also planned by Cubitt, is
really a rectangle divided by the Kings Road. In keeping
with its equally grand appearance, it has been the home
of three prime ministers: Russell, Baldwin, Chamberlain.
St. Peter's Church (1824), in the Classical-Revival style
harmonizes well. ▶ **Harrods** (1905), one of the world's
most famous department stores, with over 13 acres
of shop space; interior decoration includes Art Nouveau
tiling (main food hall) and Art Deco motifs. ▶ **Brompton
Oratory** (1884), named after the Oratory of St. Philip Neri,
Rome, was London's main Catholic church until the
opening of Westminster Cathedral (→Victoria and Pimlico); in Italian Baroque style, with statues of saints from
Siena Cathedral. ▶ Nearby is **All Saints Church** (1846-92),
with unusual facade and campanile in the style of an Italian basilica; now Russian Orthodox.   [ ]

▶ LAMBETH*

map 11-F5/Underground: Waterloo, Oval, Lambeth North.
Bus: 12, 53, 68, 188.

Lambeth was marshland until the 18thC, when London began to spread S of the Thames. Its greatest
attraction then was the Vauxhall Pleasure Gardens,
featured in many period plays, novels and pictures.
When the gardens finally disappeared in 1859, the
rest of Lambeth was a large South London suburb,
supported by such local industries as the Doulton pottery works and the railway into Waterloo (→Railway
Stations).

▶ **Lambeth Palace**, the Archbishop of Canterbury's London residence for seven centuries, and for long the only
notable building across the river from Westminster (→),
with 13thC vaulted crypt, Tudor gatehouse and great hall;
used for church functions and not generally open to the

public. ▶ Across the road, by St. Thomas's Hospital, is **Albert Embankment**, with a fine view of the Houses of Parliament (→). ▶ Beyond Westminster Bridge is **County Hall** (1919), whose future is currently in doubt after the 1986 abolition of the Greater London Council. ▶ Beyond that again is the South Bank Arts Centre (→). ▶ The **Old Vic Theatre**, Waterloo Road, opened in 1818, was distinguished by its one-time association with the Sadler's Wells opera and ballet companies (→Clerkenwell and Finsbury), and was the first home of the National Theatre (now part of the South Bank complex). ▶ In neighbouring Southwark is the Imperial War Museum (→). ▶ S of Lambeth is the famous Kennington Oval cricket ground.

▶ MADAME TUSSAUD'S AND THE LONDON PLANETARIUM*

map 4-C2/Marylebone Road. Underground: Baker Street. Bus: 30, 74, 159.

Madame Tussaud began her waxworks in Paris during the French Revolution, and opened her first London exhibition in 1835. In 1884, her grandsons moved the exhibition to the present building, where it remains the world's most famous waxworks show. The Planetarium, built on an adjoining WWII bomb site, was opened in 1958.

▶ Madame Tussaud's self-portrait. ▶ The **Grand Hall**: British monarchs, world statesmen, military leaders, writers and artists. ▶ **The Conservatory**: film and TV stars. ▶ **Superstars** from the worlds of sport and popular entertainment. ▶ The **Tableaux**, famous historical scenes, or scenes taken from pictures. ▶ The **Battle of Trafalgar**, on board *HMS Victory* and the Death of Nelson. ▶ The **Chamber of Horrors**: murderers and scenes of crime, instruments of torture and execution. ▶ **The Planetarium** (*daily ex. Christmas, 11-4.30*). ▶ The **Auditorium**, where images of stars, sun, moon, planets are projected onto a multi-dimensional screen. ▶ The **Astronomer's Gallery**, with tableaux, paintings and models tracing the history of astronomy (*Apr.-Sep.: daily, 10-6; Oct.-Mar.: daily ex. Christmas, 10-5.30*).

▶ THE MALL*

map 10-D4/Underground: Charing Cross. Bus: 3, 6, 9, 11, 12, 15, 24, 29, 53, 88, 159.

At the Restoration (1660), The Mall became a popular promenade on the N side of St. James's Park (→). The building of Nash's terraces in the early 19thC added grandeur to the scene, and it was replanned (1910) by Sir Aston Webb as a processional route from Buckingham Palace (→) to Trafalgar Square.

▶ **Admiralty Arch** (1910) marks The Mall's E end. On the S side is the rear of the Admiralty, and the WWII Citadel, a bombproof communications centre; also a statue to explorer Capt.Cook. ▶ On the N side is Nash's **Carlton House Terrace** (1837), last and grandest of his Regency projects. The one-time home of Prime Ministers Palmerston and Gladstone, the terrace now houses various institutions, including the **Institute of Contemporary Arts** (*Tue.-Sun., 12-9*), with gallery, cinema, video library, restaurant; and **The Mall Galleries** (*daily 10-5*); both have changing exhibitions. ▶ Dividing the terrace are the **Duke of York Steps** and **Memorial Column** (1834). ▶ Set back from The Mall is **St. James's Palace** (16thC), Henry VIII's Tudor residence, later modified by Wren, Gibbons, Hawksmoor, Kent; no longer a royal residence, it retains ceremonial functions: newly arrived ambassadors are 'accredited to the Court of St. James'. ▶ Facing it on

Marlborough Road is Inigo Jones' **Queen's Chapel** (1627), built for Charles I's Queen Henrietta Maria, London's earliest Classical-Revival church. ▶ Next to the palace is Nash's **Clarence House** (1825), still a royal residence; then **Lancaster House** (1825), with splendid interior decor, now a government reception and conference centre (*limited public access*). ▶ The Queen Victoria Memorial (1910) marks the W end of The Mall. ▶ **Waterloo Place** (beyond Duke of York Steps) marks the S end of Nash's Regent Street (→), with the **Guards Crimea Memorial**, partly made from captured Russian cannon, and including a statue of Florence Nightingale; also a statue to explorer Capt.Scott. ▶ A commemorative plaque marks General de Gaulle's WWII Free French HQ in Carlton Gardens. ▶ The **Athaneum** (Decimus Burton, 1828), in Classical-Revival style, is London's most distinguished club. ▶ Adjacent is **Pall Mall**, named after a popular 17thC game similar to croquet, the address of other famous clubs. ▶ **St. James's Square** (c. 1670) has the **London Library**, founded 1842 by Thomas Carlyle. The equestrian statue to William III (1808) includes the molehill that caused his fatal riding accident.   [ ]

▶ MARKETS*

Many of London's markets were regularized during the 19thC and dignified by handsome halls, galleries and arcades. Some of these, like the famous Billingsgate fish market (→City) have closed, others still flourish, with mainly wholesale but some retail outlets. More lively are the various street markets, trading in a wide variety of commodities, from oranges to antiques. Only the best known are listed here.

▶ **Leadenhall**, a mainly poultry market since the 14thC, on the site of a Roman basilica, housed in a fine Classical-Revival arcade (1881). ▶ **Smithfield**, another 14thC market dealing in cattle, established 1868 as London's premier meat market with extensive new trading halls, originally including a special station linking it with the mainline railway termini. ▶ **Spitalfields**, an old fruit and vegetable market, then one that specialized in silks at the time of Huguenot émigrés, re-opened 1928 for fruit and vegetables. ▶ **New Covent Garden**, or **Nine Elms**, moved to specially built new premises from the original Covent Garden (→) 1974, both London's and Britain's largest fruit, vegetable and flower market. ▶ **Borough**, London's oldest fruit and vegetable market, still operating. ▶ **Petticoat Lane** (Middlesex Street), most famous of London's street markets; in Victorian times it specialized in secondhand clothing; now operates on Sundays, with both clothing and food stalls. ▶ **Berwick Street**, Soho, another well-known street market for food, clothes and other domestic items. ▶ **Portobello Road** began as a Victorian street market, but since WWII has specialized in antiques and general bric-a-brac; Saturday the busiest day. ▶ **Camden Passage**, antique market in the fashionable part of Islington.   [ ]

▶ MAYFAIR*

map 4-C3/Underground: Hyde Park Corner, Marble Arch, Oxford Circus. Bus: 3, 6, 7, 12, 15, 30, 53, 74, 88, 159.

A cattle market or fair was held in the vicinity each May until the early 18thC. Residential building first started round the three main squares — Hanover, Berkeley, Grosvenor — moving London's fashionable centre of gravity N and W from Westminster (→) and the Thames (→). Most of Mayfair's great town houses have been replaced by embassies, prestige offices and salesrooms, But its excellent street plan and situation have kept it at the top of the social scale.

Street markets

You can still buy practically everything needed for everyday life (and much else besides) if you know where to look in London's street markets. These have a long and flourishing tradition, dating back to Roman times when London was established, at the lowest crossing point on the River Thames, as a trading post and a port. Numerous London street names indicate the former sites of specialist trading — Bread Street, Ironmonger Lane, Wood Street and Leather Lane tell clearly what used to be sold here. Medieval traders all dealing in one product would group together in guilds in order to protect themselves from excessive trading regulations and traffic.

The product which took up most space was the hay — in enormous quantities — needed to feed London's horses which, until the end of the last century, pulled virtually every kind of transport used in the capital. This was sold not only at Haymarket, but at Whitechapel and Smithfields too. And streets like Cheapside would have been trading centres early in London's history, for the Anglo-Saxon word 'ceap' meant 'market'.

Although many of the markets have changed their location and what they sell, the street trading tradition is still very strong. Some date from only the last ten years or less (the Hampstead Community, Jubilee and Swiss Cottage markets, for instance); some have vanished leaving streets or shops instead (Oxford Street); many sell everything as at Brick Lane, others tend to specialize: Bermondsey, Portobello and Camden Passage for antiques, Columbia Road for plants. Some are open six days a week (Chapel Street and North End Road), others take place once or twice a week (Brick Lane).

Markets have always reflected the character of the surrounding inhabitants, and while Petticoat Lane is a traditionally Jewish area connected with the rag trade (clothes), many of the other East London markets now have a distinctively Asian flavour, while South London's Brixton market offers an exotic range of Caribbean fruits, vegetables, fish and other food unknown elsewhere in London, resounding to the noise of reggae records which are also for sale.

▶ **Park Lane**, running along the E side of Hyde Park (→) has some of London's most famous hotels — Grosvenor House, The Dorchester and the tall London Hilton (1963). A few elegant town houses facing the park remain. ▶ **Curzon Street** has Georgian terraced houses; also Crewe House (1730) in its own grounds; and almost opposite, **Shepherd Market**, named after architect Edward Shepherd, an enclave of small shops, restaurants and pubs. ▶ **The Royal Institution**, Albermarle Street, has the **Michael Faraday Museum** (*Tue.-Thu., 1-4; Cl. Bank Hols.*), a restoration of the scientist's laboratory. ▶ **Berkeley Square** has 18th and 19thC houses on its W side. ▶ The **Church of the Immaculate Conception** (1844), Farm Street, headquarters of the English Jesuits, has a notable Gothic-Revival interior and high altar by Pugin. ▶ **Grosvenor Chapel** (1739), South Audley Street, is in American colonial style. ▶ **Grosvenor Square** (1731), one of London's largest, was for long its most exclusive address. In WWII no. 20 was General Eisenhower's headquarters, and the American connection remains, with the U.S. Embassy (1959) and statue to President Roosevelt (1948). ▶ **Hanover Square** (1720) E of Bond Street (→), is named after George I, formerly Elector of Hanover. The

Hanover Square Rooms (demolished 1900), on the E side, were London's premier concert hall, where J.C. Bach, Haydn, Paganini and Liszt all performed. ▶ **St. George's Church** (1724), just to the S, has seen many famous weddings — Lady Hamilton, Shelley, Disraeli, George Eliot, Asquith; two cast-iron dogs in the porch are a notable feature.   [ ]

▶ NATIONAL GALLERY*

map 5-E3/Trafalgar Square. Underground: Charing Cross. Bus: 3, 6, 9, 11, 12, 15, 24, 29, 53, 88, 159.

Founded 1824, with a nucleus of 38 pictures, the National Gallery now houses the nation's most valuable collection of over 2000 paintings, from early Italian Renaissance to French post-Impressionism. The building, on the N side of Trafalgar Square, was designed by William Wilkins (1838). There have been several extensions, and another is planned.

▶ Early Italian Renaissance — Duccio, Masaccio, Uccello (*Battle of San Romano*), Piero della Francesca (*Baptism of Christ*), Mantegna, Bellini, Botticelli (rooms 1-6, 10-13). ▶ High Renaissance — Leonardo da Vinci (cartoon, *The Virgin and Child*), Raphael, Michelangelo, Titian (*Bacchus and Ariadne*), Tintoretto, Veronese (rooms 7-9, 14, 30). Early Northern School — Van Eyck, Bosch, Brueghel, Dürer, Holbein (*The Ambassadors*; rooms 23-25). Dutch and Flemish Schools — Frans Hals, Rembrandt (*Self-Portrait*), Vermeer, de Hooch, Rubens (*Portrait, The Straw Hat*), Van Dyck (*Equestrian Portrait of Charles I*; rooms 15-22, 27, 28). ▶ Italian and French Schools, 17th/18thC — Caravaggio, Giordano, Tiepolo, Canaletto, Poussin, Claude (rooms 29, 32-34). Spanish School — El Greco, Velasquez (*The Toilet of Venus*), Murillo, Goya (rooms 41, 42). ▶ British School — Hogarth, Gainsborough, Reynolds, Stubbs, Constable (*The Hay Wain*), Turner (*The Fighting Temeraire*; rooms 35, 36, 38, 39). ▶ French Impressionist and post-Impressionist — Manet, Degas, Cezanne (*Bathers*), Monet, Renoir, Seurat, Van Gogh (*Sunflowers*; rooms 40, 43, 46; *Mon.-Sat., 10-5.30, Sun., 2-5.30; Cl. I Jan., Good Fri., May Day, 24-26 Dec.*).   [ ]

▶ NATIONAL PORTRAIT GALLERY*

map 5-E3/St. Martins Place. Underground: Charing Cross, Leicester Square. Bus: 3, 6, 9, 11,12, 15, 24, 29, 53, 88, 159.

Founded in 1856, the gallery moved to its present building, at the rear of the National Gallery (→), in 1895. It has over 8000 portraits, cartoons and caricatures of famous British men and women, from Tudor times to the present day. There are also many portrait photographs.

▶ Henry VII, Henry VIII, Sir Thomas More by Hobein; Gladstone and Disraeli by Millais; self-portraits by Hogarth, Reynolds, Gainsborough; the Bronte Sisters by brother Branwell; Sir Winston Churchill by Sickert; T.S. Eliot by Epstein (*Mon.-Fri., 10-5, Sat., 10-6, Sun., 2-6; Cl. I Jan., Good Fri., May Day, 24-26 Dec.*).   [ ]

▶ NATURAL HISTORY MUSEUM*

map 8-A4/Cromwell Road. Underground: South Kensington. Bus: 14, 30, 74.

In 1881 the natural history section of the British Museum (→) moved to its new premises in South Kensington. The building, by Alfred Waterhouse, is the most colourful and fanciful of all London's museums. It has accumulated some 40 million specimens (many of them insects), the collection growing annually by about 300,000 specimens.

▶ Ground floor: dinosaurs and their living relatives. Central Hall: fossil mammals; fossil invertebrates and fishes; birds, insects, spiders; whales; human biology; ecology and wildlife in danger. ▶ First floor: Darwin and The Origin of Species ; ▶ Man's place in evolution. ▶ Second floor: British natural history. (*Mon.-Sat., 10-6, Sun., 2.30-6; Cl. I Jan., Good Fri., May Day, 24-26 Dec.*).

▶ OSTERLEY HOUSE*

map p. 96-A1/Thornbury Road. Underground: Osterley.

Set in extensive parkland in West London, Osterley House was originally built by Sir Thomas Gresham, financier to Elizabeth I. It was remodeled several times, most notably by Robert Adam (1763-7), the interior decoration being one of the finest achievements.

▶ The most notable exterior feature is Adam's Greek-Ionic double entrance portico; **entrance hall** with double apse, ceiling with floral scrolls, marble floor; **drawing room**, rich in gilding and other ornamentation, with French Neoclassical sofas and chairs; **library** with furniture and fittings by John Linnell, leading 18thC cabinet-maker; **tapestry room** with Adam motifs, very fine Gobelin tapestries and chairs in matching style (*Apr.-Sep.: Tue.-Sun., 2-6; Oct.-Mar.: Tue.-Sun., 12-4; Cl. I Jan., Good Fri., May Day, 24-26 Dec.*).

▶ OXFORD STREET AND BOND STREET

map 4-C-D3/Underground: Marble Arch, Bond Street, Oxford Circus. Bus: 6, 7, 12, 15, 30, 73, 74, 88, 159.

Oxford Street, dividing Mayfair (→) from Marylebone to the N, was for long known as Tyburn Way, leading to the public place of execution at its W end (now Marble Arch). Though the start of a one-time road to Oxford, it takes its name from the Earl of Oxford, who began its 18thC development. By the end of the 19thC it was London's principal shopping street. Bond Street (Old and New), named after Sir Thomas Bond, 17thC court financier, and the home of William Pitt the Elder, Lord Nelson and Lady Hamilton, is the capital's most exclusive centre for luxury goods and antiques.

▶ Oxford Street's largest department store is **Selfridge's**, built 1909 by American businessman Gordon Selfridge, in massive Greek-Revival style, with clock and figure ('The Queen of Time') over the main entrance; famous for its Christmas window displays. ▶ Two other leading stores are D.H. Evans and John Lewis. ▶ **Sotheby's** (Sotheby Parke Bernet) of New Bond Street, world-famous fine art auctioneers, was founded in 1744, and moved to its present address in 1917; the sculpture over the door is Egyptian (c. 1600 B.C.). ▶ On N side of Oxford Street, **St. Peter's Church**, Vere Street (1721): windows by Burne-Jones. ▶ **Portman Square** (1764) has the **Courtauld Institute of Art** (Robert Adam, 1775). ▶ In **Cavendish Square** (1717) is the **Convent of the Holy Child**, with Epstein's sculpture *Madonna and Child* (1953) over the entrance. ▶ Linking the two squares is Wigmore Street, with the Wigmore (formerly Bechstein) Hall concert room. ▶ Just off Baker Street is Manchester Square and the Wallace Collection (→).

▶ PICCADILLY AND HAYMARKET*

map 5-D3/Underground: Green Park, Piccadilly Circus.
Bus: 3, 6, 9, 14, 15, 19, 22, 53, 88, 159.

Piccadilly owes its name to a 17thC dressmaker who grew rich making a type of frilly collar called a 'picadil', and built a house in the vicinity. The thoroughfare, with Green Park on the S side for much of its length, was largely developed by the mid-18thC, with some of London's most palatial homes. Increasing traffic turned it from a residential street into the main commercial artery of London's West End. The Haymarket, a wide street of theatres and cinemas, was once a hay, straw and cattle market. The two thoroughfares encompass the area of St. James's, with its famous clubs.

▶ **Green Park**, with Piccadilly on the N side and Constitution Hill on the S, has seen some famous events, notably the fireworks display celebrating the Peace of Aix-la-Chapelle (1748), for which Handel wrote his Royal Fireworks Music. ▶ By the park's NE corner is the **Ritz Hotel** (1906) in opulent French Empire style. ▶ Running from Piccadilly is **St. James's Street** with some famous London clubs: Boodle's (1765), Brook's (1778) and White's (1788). ▶ **Jermyn Street**, S of and parallel to Piccadilly, has some of London's oldest-established shops. **Piccadilly Arcade** connects the two streets. ▶ The oldest-established shop in Piccadilly itself is **Fortnum and Mason**, founded 1705. ▶ **St. James's Church**, Piccadilly (Wren, 1684) has a large, handsome interior, with reredos, font and organ case by Grinling Gibbons; attached to it is the **London Brass Rubbing Centre** (*Mon.-Sat., 10-6, Sun., 12-6*), with replica brasses from many churches. ▶ On Piccadilly's N side is **Burlington House** (1717 with extensions), home of the Royal Academy, the nation's oldest fine arts society, founded 1768 (*daily 10-6; Cl. Good Fri., Christmas*). Its permanent collection has paintings by Reynolds, Gainsborough, Stubbs, Turner and sculpture by Michelangelo; changing exhibitions throughout the year, including the famous Summer Exhibition. ▶ Behind Burlington House, in Burlington Gardens, is **The Museum of Mankind** (*Mon.-Sat., 10-5, Sun., 2.30-6; Cl. I Jan., Good Fri., May Day, 24-27 Dec.*), a branch of the British Museum (→), with ethnic exhibits from around the world. ▶ On the E side of Burlington House is **The Albany** (1774), one of Piccadilly's original residences, the address of many celebrities. ▶ On the other side is **Burlington Arcade** (1819). ▶ **Piccadilly Circus**, at the junction of Piccadilly, Regent Street (→) and Shaftesbury Avenue, is the hub of London's theatreland. Its most famous feature is the fountain and statue of **Eros**, erected 1893 as a memorial to philanthropist Lord Shaftesbury, and recently resited as part of a new traffic scheme. ▶ Neighbouring **Leicester Square**, once a residential precinct with statues ranging from Shakespeare to Charlie Chaplin and several big cinemas. ▶ The **Theatre Royal**, Haymarket (Nash, 1831), with Corinthian-Greek portico, is one of London's most handsome buildings. ▶ Facing it is **Her Majesty's Theatre**, the fourth such building on the site, behind which is the **Royal Opera Arcade** (Nash, 1818), London's earliest shopping arcade.

▶ PUBS*

Underground: Blackfriars, St. Paul's, Mansion House, Bank, Monument, Aldgate. Bus: 6, 9, 11, 15.

The City has nearly 200 public houses and wine bars — many catering for the working population and closed at weekends. All are in the tradition of British pubs, often places of strong local character. Some of the best known also enshrine as much of its history.

Coffee houses

An exotic new drink was brought to England in the 17thC: it had arrived in Europe from Arabia and was an infusion of coffee beans. The first coffee house was actually set up in Oxford, but in 1652, London's Cornhill had its own establishment in St. Michael's Alley. Soon there were many coffee houses in the city — along the Strand and Fleet Street. The new drink was supposed to be beneficial to the health — and to cure the effects of too many hours spent in the tavern. It certainly appeared to encourage conversations. In the club-like atmosphere of the coffee houses, men would meet to discuss politics, literature and gossip. Chocolate, imported from the West Indies, was soon drunk in similar surroundings. Distinguished men of the day such as Dr. Johnson, Samuel Pepys, David Garrick, Joseph Addison and Richard Steele frequented such places and in time the coffee and chocolate houses developed their specialist interests from the subjects discussed there. The Tatler magazine, founded by Steele in 1709, first reported 'entertainment' from White's Chocolate House, 'poetry' from Will's Coffee House, and 'foreign and domestic news' from St. James's Coffee House. The Spectator was brought out by Steele and Addison shortly afterwards. Newspapers printed in relatively small quantities were circulated among the coffee and chocolate drinkers, and gradually newspaper offices crowded out the coffee houses in Fleet Street. Business talk at Lloyd's coffee house became a business in itself as Lloyd's became and remained one of the most important names in the world of insurance, and establishments like White's Chocolate House developed into the select gentlemen's clubs they are today.

▶ **Cock Tavern**, Fleet Street, with reminders of Pepys and of its days as a chop house frequented by Dickens. ▶ **Cheshire Cheese**, Fleet Street, largely 17thC oak-beamed building, also with a literary past — Johnson, Boswell, Dickens, Thackeray, Conan Doyle. ▶ Between them is **El Vino's** wine bar, traditional haunt of journalists, where women were not served until 1982. ▶ **Punch Tavern**, with original drawings and cartoons from *Punch* magazine. ▶ **Magpie and Stump**, facing the Central Criminal Court (Old Bailey), with memories of Newgate Prison and public executions. ▶ **Olde Watling**, built by Wren and frequented by him during work on St. Paul's; named after the Roman road on which it stands. ▶ **Samuel Pepys**, in a Thames wharf, with mementoes of the diarist. ▶ **Williamson's Tavern**, 17thC, one-time residence of Lord Mayors, visited by William and Mary, with wrought-iron gates commemorating this; a stone marks the City centre. ▶ **Olde Dr Butler's Head**, restored 17thC; named after a quack physician to James I. ▶ **George and Vulture**, restored 18thC, associated with Dickens' *Pickwick Papers*. ▶ **Jamaica Wine House**, probably also London's first coffee house. ▶ **Square Rigger**, furnished in the style of an 18thC sailing ship. ▶ **Olde Wine Shades**, wine bar founded 1663, with relics of its past. ▶ **Hoop and Grapes**: 13thC foundations, mostly 17thC restored; oldest City pub with many relics.

▶ RAILWAY STATIONS*

Britain led the world in railway construction, the first in London being the Greenwich to London Bridge

railway (1836). Soon after, railway companies started building terminus stations linking London with the
rest of the country, completely changing the capital's
appearance and character in the process. The number of companies and the intense competition
between them explain the large number of stations,
even for a city of London's size. Some are of outstanding architectural and engineering interest.

▶ **Euston** (1968), London's newest mainline station, but
on the site of Robert Stephenson's original 1837 station, and near the historic spot where Richard Tevithick
demonstrated his pioneer steam locomotive 'Catch Me
Who Can' in 1808. ▶ Near neighbours along the Euston
Road are **Kings Cross** (1851), whose handsome structure
remains virtually intact, though obscured by the approach,
and **St. Pancras**, notable for its arched roof (1866), once
the world's widest single span (245 ft.), and for Sir George
Gilbert Scott's massive Gothic-Revival hotel and offices
(1872). ▶ **Paddington's** splendid triple-arch iron and glass
roof (1851) is the work of Isambard Kingdom Brunel; the
adjoining hotel (Philip Hardwick, 1854) is equally grand
inside. ▶ **Victoria**, long known as 'The Gateway to the
Continent', the main rail link between London and the
rest of Europe, was the scene of many ceremonial arrivals
and departures; adjoining Grosvenor Hotel (1861) is cor-
respondingly opulent. ▶ **Waterloo**, the largest after construction (1900-22), was originally planned to continue
across the river into the City. In 1854 there was an adjacent station — long since demolished — serving a fashionable country cemetery, called the Necropolis Station.
▶ Large and busy **Liverpool Street**, **Cannon Street**, with
imposing twin towers and above the river, **Blackfriars**,
Holborn Viaduct and **Fenchurch Street** all penetrate the
City. ▶ There are also **Charing Cross**, with another grand
Victorian hotel and in the forecourt, a replica of the cross
marking the resting place of a queen before burial in
Westminster Abbey; **London Bridge**, the oldest in origin;
and **Marylebone** (1899).

▶ REGENT'S PARK**

map 4-C2/Underground: Baker Street, Regent's Park.
Bus: 30, 74, 159.

Like most of London's other royal parks, Regent's
Park was a hunting reserve. Its transformation dates
from 1811, when John Nash, with backing from the
Prince Regent (George IV), drew up plans to turn it
into a luxurious residential estate or garden suburb.
The result is the magnificent group of terraces along
much of the park's perimeter, plus Park Crescent,
leading to Portland Place and Regent Street (→).

▶ The grandest Regency terraces are **Chester** (1825) and
Cumberland (1826) on the E side of the park, and **Hanover** (1823) on the W. ▶ Next to Hanover Terrace is the
equally striking **Mosque** (1977), with the Islamic Cultural
Centre adjoining. ▶ The Inner Circle road was a part of
Nash's original plan; it now encloses **Queen Mary's Garden** with fountain, pond, rose garden and restaurant, also
the **Open Air Theatre**, first opened in 1933 for summer
seasons, mainly of Shakespeare. ▶ Also by the Inner
Circle is Bedford College, with an annexe in The Holme
(Decimus Burton, 1819). ▶ The boating lake is also a part
of Nash's original plan. ▶ The N side of the park is
largely given over to the **Zoological Gardens** (*Mar.-Oct.:
9-6, daily; Nov.-Feb.: 10-6; Cl. Christmas*), founded 1826
and expanded from its original 5-acre site to the present
36 acres, with well over 1000 species of mammal, bird,
reptile, fish and insect. The Zoological Society of London
is a world centre of scientific study and research.

Nearby

▶ Near the park, in Marylebone Road, is Madame Tussaud's and the London Planetarium (→). ▶ In neighbouring Baker Street are the offices of the Abbey National

building society, on the site of what was the home of fictional detective Sherlock Holmes (no. 221B). ▶ By the W side of the park, facing Park Road, is **St. John's Wood Chapel** (Thomas Hardwick, 1813), and beyond that, **Lord's Cricket Ground**, headquarters of the MCC. The **Cricket Memorial Gallery** (*open match days 10.30-5, or by prior appointment*) has the famous Ashes trophy and other cricketing memorabilia. ▶ N of the park, in Regent's Park Road., is **Cecil Sharp House** (*Mon.-Fri., 9.30-5.30*), headquarters of the English Folk Song and Dance Society, with the **Vaughan Williams Memorial Library**.

▶ REGENT STREET*

map 4-D3/Underground: Oxford Circus, Piccadilly Circus. Bus: 3, 6, 7, 9, 12, 14, 15, 19, 22, 53, 73, 88, 159.

This was part of John Nash's grand design (1811) linking Regent's Park (→), via Portland Place, with Carlton House, the Prince Regent's former palace on The Mall (→), at the same time creating a new NS thoroughfare for fashionable West London. Nash's own colonnaded section, called The Quadrant, was modified in 1848, and more changes were made from then on, until almost the entire street was rebuilt in the 1920s, creating the major shopping centre of today.

▶ At the meeting of Portland Place and Upper Regent Street is **Broadcasting House** (1931), with extensions, the BBC's main administrative and sound broadcasting centre. ▶ Next to it is **All Souls Church**, Langham Place (Nash, 1824), situated at a strategic point in Nash's original plan, and most original in design, with its conical portico and conical spire; bust of the architect by the entrance. ▶ Just S of Oxford Circus is Liberty's department store (1924-6): front section is in Neoclassical style, the slightly earlier part, in adjoining Great Marlborough Street, in mock-Tudor, with oak beams taken from two old sailing ships. Next to it is **Dickens and Jones** department store. ▶ On the N side of The Quadrant is the **Cafe Royal**, founded 1865, frequented by royalty and other celebrities. ▶ Further round The Quadrant are other famous London stores: Austin Reed, Aquascutum, Mappin and Webb (goldsmiths, silversmiths, jewelers).

▶ RICHMOND**

map p. 96-A2/Underground: Richmond. British Rail: Richmond. Bus: 65, 71.

Richmond-on-Thames owes its name to Henry VII, who built a palace there, naming it Rychemond, after his estates in Yorkshire. The town prospered, thanks to his palace, its strategic position to other royal homes, at Kew (→), Hampton Court (→) and Windsor, and to its own attractive site. The coming of the railway brought fresh prosperity in the form of residential development. Together with its neighbouring park, it is one of London's most popular recreational areas.

▶ **The Green**, a Tudor jousting ground, retains many fine Georgian houses, notably those in **Maids of Honour Row**. The **Richmond Theatre** (1899) symbolizes the Green's theatrical past, marked by such figures as David Garrick, Edmund Kean and Mrs Siddons. ▶ Nearby are reminders of the **palace** (mostly destroyed during the Civil War), including the **gateway**, with Henry VII's coat-of-arms, the **Wardrobe** building, and the handsomely converted **Trumpeter's House** (once the home of Austrian statesman Metternich). ▶ By the river is **Asgill House** (1760), home of a past Lord Mayor of London. ▶ **Richmond Bridge** (1774), though widened, retains its charm. ▶ Beyond the railway and Twickenham bridges is Richmond lock and foot-bridge. ▶ The parish church of **St. Mary Magdalene** is mainly Tudor, with some fine brasses and monuments (including one to Edmund Kean). ▶ **Richmond Hill** commands a splendid view of the river and Petersham meadows, much admired by Turner. **Wick House** (1771) was the home of Joshua Reynolds, who also painted the scene. ▶ **Richmond Park**, enclosed as a hunting reserve by Charles I, is the largest of the royal parks (2470 acres), noted for its deer and other wildlife, and for its ancient groves of oak trees. ▶ The **Isabella Plantation** has a profusion of shrubs and flowers. ▶ The top of **Sawyer's Hill**, near Richmond Gate, has a view of St. Paul's and the city of London to the E, and of Windsor Castle to the NW ▶ Two notable buildings in the park are **White Lodge** (1727), now a part of the Royal Ballet School and **Thatched House Lodge** (1670), a royal residence. A third, **Pembroke Lodge**, with surrounding gardens, is a cafeteria restaurant. Buses: 65, 71. ▶ A walk upstream, or a short bus ride, is Ham House (1610; *Apr.-Sep.: Tue.-Sun., 2-6; Oct.-Mar., Tue.-Sun., 12-4*): Jacobean furnishings, paintings, tapestries and gardens laid out in the same period style.   ⊔⊔

▶ SCIENCE MUSEUM*

map 8-B4/Underground: South Kensington. Bus: 14, 30, 74.

The collection grew in a haphazard way from the middle of the 19thC, but now comprises Britain's foremost museum of science and industry. The building (1913), designed like a big department store, is ideal for the many large exhibits. An extension, connected with the Imperial College of Science and Technology, houses the museum's libary (*Mon.-Sat., 10-5.30; Cl. Bank Hols.*).

▶ Ground floor: **Foucault's Pendulum**, registered the earth's rotation (by the main entrance); motive power, stationary steam engines, steam turbines, hot air, gas and oil engines (galleries 2, 3, 5); rail transport, early steam locomotives, rail equipment, electric traction (galleries 7, 8); road transport, early motor cars, gas-turbine vehicles, motor cycles (galleries 7-10). ▶ First floor: telecommunications (galleries 20, 25); iron and steel (gallery 22); textiles and plastics (galleries 24, 25); gas industry (gallery 26); astronomy, telescopes, terrestrial and celestial globes, orreries (gallery 30). ▶ Second floor: chemistry, history and industries (galleries 41-43, 45); nuclear physics and power (gallery 44); computers (gallery 46). ▶ Third floor: photography and cinematography (gallery 60); electricity and magnetism (gallery 64); aeronautics (gallery 68, 69). ▶ Fourth and fifth floors: Wellcome Museum of History of Medicine (*Mon.-Sat., 10-6, Sun., 2.30-6; Cl. I Jan., Good Fri., May Day, 24-26 Dec.*). ⊔⊔

▶ SOHO*

map 5-D3/Underground: Piccadilly Circus, Leicester Square, Oxford Circus, Tottenham Court Road. Bus: 3, 6, 7, 12, 14, 15, 19, 22, 24, 29, 53, 73, 88, 159.

The name of this most compact and cosmopolitan of all London districts is probably derived from the old hunting cry 'So-Ho', though the area was already quite urban by the 17thC. French Huguenots were among the first to settle there, followed by Italians, Greeks, Chinese and people of many other races and nationalities. From a peak in the 19thC, the resident population has dropped to less than 3000. Most now go there to work, or to seek diversion in its theatres, cinemas, restaurants, nightclubs and sex shops.

The Docklands

London's docks have taken on a new aspect. With the end of Britain's overseas empire, the bombing of World War II and modern means of transport, the once-thriving London docks fell into disrepair. In 1965 a semi-public organization, the London Docklands Development Corporation, was formed to renovate this ancient port on the Thames. This renovation was effected in a grandiose manner. Office buildings shopping centers, luxury apartments and industria workspace were designed, and, in order to maintair a sense of the area's character, marinas for pleasure boats were constructed. The Docklands became a city within a city. This new area needed new means of transportation. Accordingly, new roads were laid out, highway links, rail links and boat links were created. The most impressive innovation, however, was the construction of a new airport — right in the center of London. 10 kilometres from the City', London City Airport (Stolport) opened in 1987 and is well-placed to shuttle businessmen to and from the Continent and to other cities in Britain.

▶ **Shaftesbury Avenue** (1886) is noted for its theatres — Apollo, Globe, Lyric, Palace, Queen's Saville. ▶ The **Windmill Theatre**, Great Windmill Street, is famous as the only London theatre to remain open throughout WWII, with its slogan 'We never closed'. ▶ Between Shaftesbury Avenue and Leicester Square, the **Church of Notre Dame de France** (1955), replacing an earlier edifice bombed in WWII, is largely circular, with decoration by Jean Cocteau, including an Aubusson tapestry. ▶ In the vicinity of Golden Square is the **Church of Our Lady of the Assumption**, Warwick Street; also **Carnaby Street** (→). ▶ The **Palladium**, Argyll Street, just off Oxford Circus, is London's chief variety theatre. ▶ Wardour Street and Dean Street are commercial centres of the cinema industry. ▶ **Ronnie Scott's**, Frith Street, is London's premier jazz club. ▶ **Soho Square** (c. 1680) has a statue to Charles II and two churches, **St. Patrick's Roman Catholic Church**, and the **French Protestant Church**, a reminder of Soho's Huguenot past. ▶ On the other side of Charing Cross Road, just outside Soho proper, is the church of **St. Giles-in-the-Fields** (1733), on the site of an earlier church and leper hospital. The Great Plague of 1665 started in the parish. □

▶ SOUTH BANK ARTS CENTRE*

map 5-E3/Underground: Waterloo. Bus: 68, 188.

The genesis of the South Bank, as it is generally known, was the 1951 Festival of Britain, when a semi-derelict industrial area of Lambeth riverside, around Hungerford Railway Bridge and Waterloo Bridge, was chosen for the festival's main exhibition site. A new concert hall, the Royal Festival Hall, was included, and from this the rest of the Arts Centre, unified by a large pedestrian precinct, has grown.

▶ **Royal Festival Hall** (1951, enlarged 1965), with year-round concert and ballet seasons, plus riverside restaurant, cafeterias and bars, bookshop, art exhibitions, and fine panorama of London across the river. ▶ **Queen Elizabeth** and **Purcell Rooms** (1967), complementing the Festival Hall as smaller concert or recital rooms. ▶ **Hayward Gallery** (1968), in the same building complex, stages major art exhibitions. ▶ **National Film Theatre**, beneath Waterloo Bridge, first opened 1951 and enlarged 1970, with two cinemas and a cinema museum in preparation. ▶ On the other side of Waterloo Bridge, the **Nation-**

al Theatre complex (1977) has three theatres: Olivier (the largest), Lyttleton and Cottesloe, plus bookshops, restaurant, cafeterias and striking **views** across the Thames.

▶ SOUTHWARK*

map 12-F-G4/Underground: London Bridge, Borough. British Rail: London Bridge.

Southwark, or South Work, is the oldest part of London S of the Thames, by the main route from the Continent into the City (→) over London Bridge. Hence its many coaching inns. Also, with more space than the City, it became a place of entertainment (Shakespeare's Globe Theatre and the Bear Garden) and of prisons (notably the Clink and Marshalsea). There is still much evidence of this long and colourful past in this bustling S London district today.

▶ **Southwark Cathedral** (St. Saviour's) by the approach to London Bridge. Founded as a priory 1106, most of the edifice dates from the 15thC — London's earliest Gothic church — the square tower being of later date; it became a cathedral only in 1905. The interior is rich in decoration and in **monuments**: wooden effigy of a knight (c. 1275), the memorial to John Gower (friend of the poet Chaucer) and Shakespeare (1912); **Harvard Chapel**, in honour of John Harvard, baptized in the church and founder of America's Harvard University. ▶ Just E of the cathedral is Guy's Hospital, founded 1722, with large modern extensions; the **old operating theatre** in Thomas Street may still be visited (*Mon., Wed., Fri., 12.30-4*). ▶ Under the arches of London Bridge Station is the **London Dungeon** (*Apr.-Sep.: daily 10-5.45; Oct.-Mar.: daily 10-4.30*), a museum of the macabre. ▶ In Borough High Street are reminders of several coaching inns, including the **George Inn** (1676), with surviving galleries and courtyard. ▶ W of the cathedral is **St. Mary Overie's Dock**, containing an old merchant ship; and the remains of Winchester House (c. 1100). ▶ Beyond Clink Street, and traversed by Southwark Bridge, is the area of Bankside, dominated by the power station (1929, Giles Gilbert Scott) now abandoned. ▶ Close by is the site of the Globe Theatre (with plans for its reconstruction) and the **Bear Gardens Museum** (*Tue.-Sat., 10-5.30, Sun., 2-6; Cl. 25-26 Dec. I Jan.*), tracing the history of Elizabethan theatre, with models of the Globe and Cockpit playhouses. ▶ The 18thC **Anchor Inn** has relics of the old Clink Prison. ▶ The **Church of St. George the Martyr** (founded 1122, rebuilt 1736): interesting interior, including memorials to city livery companies and to Dickens' novel *Little Dorrit*, inspired by the nearby Marshalsea debtors' prison.

▶ ST. JAMES'S PARK*

map 10-D4/Underground: St. James's Park.

Originally the garden of a leper hospital, St. James's Park is the oldest of London's royal parks and a particular favourite of Charles II who created the lake, famous for its wildfowl. It is a beautiful and tranquil place despite being at the heart of the city.

▶ The **view** from the footbridge across the lake, E to Whitehall (→) and W to Buckingham Palace (→), is one of the most picturesque in London. ▶ At the E end, facing **Horse Guards Parade**, is the **Guards Memorial** (1926). ▶ The park is bordered, on the N side, by The Mall (→), and on the S by **Birdcage Walk** which takes its name from the aviary kept there by Charles II. ▶ By Birdcage Walk are the renovated **Wellington Barracks** (1833) and new **Guards Chapel** (1963). ▶ Just behind Birdcage Walk and the bronze sculpture, *Mother and Child*, by Henry Moore, is **Queen Anne's Gate**, a beautifully preserved enclave of 18thC houses with a statue to the monarch.

Dick Whittington

The legend of Dick Whittington may be far from the truth, but it was certainly based on a real person who lived in London during the 14thC. According to the story, Dick was a poor boy who came to London to seek his fortune having been told that the streets were paved with gold. He found a job in the house of an Alderman Fitz-Warren, but was so harshly treated by the cook there that he ran away. However, as he walked up Highgate Hill, he heard Bow Bells chiming 'Turn again, Whittington, thrice Mayor of London'. Encouraged by this prophecy, he returned. All he possessed in the world was a cat, but this creature made him a fortune, and he married Alice, daughter of his master.

There was indeed a Richard Whittington who was born around 1358 and died in 1423, no poor boy but the son of Sir William Whittington. Nevertheless, he was apprenticed to Fitz-Warren, a prosperous mercer, and married his daughter. Moreover, he did become Mayor — not just once, but four times — as well as being a Member of Parliament. There is no specific record of his cat, but a sculpted stone of him holding a cat was discovered in the foundations of a 15thC house belonging to his family. He had no children, but left his great wealth to charity. During his lifetime he was renowned for his generosity and honesty. He was a member of the mercers' company and attacked bad practice among city merchants; he founded libraries, almshouses, helped individuals in need, restored St. Bartholemew's Hospital, entertained the king and gave him money. A stone set up on Highgate Hill in 1821 marks the spot where the young Richard is supposed to have sat when he heard Bow Bells calling him.

▶ ST. PAUL'S CATHEDRAL***

map 6-G3/Underground: St. Paul's, Mansion House. Bus: 6, 9, 11, 15.

The present building owes its existence to the Great Fire of 1666, which destroyed most of the Norman-Gothic cathedral. It was conceived by Sir Christopher Wren as the centrepiece of a new plan for the whole City of London after the fire. Work began on the great Renaissance-style building in 1675, and was finished in 1711, when the last stone in the lantern above the dome was set in place by the 79-year-old architect's son. It was damaged during WWII, but saved from destruction by a special corps of fire-watchers. It has been the setting of many big state occasions, including the funerals of Nelson (1806), Wellington (1852), Sir Winston Churchill (1965) and the Wedding of Prince Charles to Lady Diana Spencer (1981).

▶ The most striking external feature is the **dome**, mounted on its pillared 'drum' and surmounted by the lantern and golden cross, 365 ft. above ground level. ▶ The twin towers on the W front were a last-minute addition by Wren, the S tower with a clock and the bell known as 'Great Tom', the N tower with a peal of bells, which ring each Sunday. ▶ The whole exterior is richly decorated with stone statues and reliefs by Grinling Gibbons and others. ▶ The main interior decoration is the **frescoes** round the vault of the dome, by James Thornhill, the **choir stalls** and **organ case** by Gibbons, wrought-iron **railings**, **gates** and **screens** by French iron-worker Jean Tijou, and the more recent **mosaics** above the choir. ▶ In the nave, transepts and choir are **monuments** to Nelson, Wellington and John Donne, poet and Dean of old St. Paul's, portrayed in his funeral shroud. ▶ Holman Hunt's painting, *Light of the World*, hangs in the S aisle. ▶ **The American Chapel**, commemorating the dead of WWII, is behind the new High Altar, which commemorates the British Commonwealth dead of two World Wars. ▶ Buried in the **crypt** (*Cl. Sun. and some other days*) is Wren himself; also Nelson and Wellington, whose funeral gun carriage reposes here. There are many other monuments or memorial plaques to famous British men and women. ▶ Access to the internal **Whispering Gallery**, and to the external galleries around the dome and, above it, the **Golden Gallery**, 542 steps from the ground (*Mon.-Sat.: summer 9-6, 5 in winter; Sun.: services only*).   [ ]

▶ STRAND, ALDWYCH AND EMBANKMENT*

map 5-E3/Underground: Charing Cross, Aldwych, Embankment. Bus: 3, 6, 9, 11, 12, 15, 23, 29, 53, 68, 88, 159, 188.

The Strand was originally a bridle path along the N side of the Thames. As a link between the City (→) and Westminster (→) — today between Fleet Street and Trafalgar Square — it was important from the 13thC on, first as a place of large houses for the nobility and clergy, and from the 17thC to the present day as an area largely devoted to commerce and entertainment. The Embankment, properly the Victoria Embankment (1864-70), is the main part of the greatest of London's 19thC public works, reclaiming acres of riverside and mud and creating a new N bank for the Thames. It is a vital road link between the City, Westminster, Victoria (→) and Chelsea (→).

▶ By St. Martin's Lane is the church of **St. Martin-in-the-Fields** (James Gibbs, 1724), burial place of Nell Gwynne, highwayman Jack Sheppard, Hogarth, Reynolds and Thomas Chippendale; also associated with charity work and with a London orchestra. ▶ In St. Martin's Lane is **The Coliseum**, home of the English National Opera and **Duke of York's Theatre**. ▶ On the N side of the Strand are the **Adelphi** and **Vaudeville** theatres and Strand Palace Hotel (1930). ▶ On the S side is the **Savoy Hotel**, London's most luxurious when opened by impresario Richard D'Oyly Carte in 1889, with the celebrated Auguste Escoffier as chef. ▶ Adjoining Savoy Theatre (1881, reconstructed 1929), also financed by D'Oyly Carte, saw the first production of most of the Gilbert and Sullivan operettas. ▶ **Savoy Chapel**, chapel of the Royal Victorian Order, dates back to the 16thC but is mostly of much more recent date. ▶ Savoy Hill, first premises of the BBC, is commemorated by a plaque (no. 2 Savoy Place). ▶ By the E side of Waterloo Bridge (Lancaster Place) is Somerset House (Sir William Chambers, 1776-86), occupied mainly by government offices. On the site of an earlier palace, it is one of London's grandest Classical-Revival buildings, originally with a river frontage, and still with an imposing riverside façade. The E wing (Robert Smirke, 1835) houses King's College, now a part of London University. ▶ In Strand Lane is the so-called Roman Bath, though its authenticity is doubtful. ▶ Aldwych, opened 1905, links Kingsway with the Strand. The Strand and Aldwych theatres and Waldorf Hotel are on the N side. On the S side is Bush House (1935), home of BBC overseas services, flanked by India House and Australia House. ▶ Continuing in the Strand itself, on island sites, are the churches of **St. Mary-le-Strand** (1717) and **St. Clement Danes** (Wren, 1682), largely destroyed in WWII and reconstructed, 1955, as a RAF memorial church. A bronze statue of Dr. Johnson (1910) faces Fleet Street. ▶ Marking the Strand's link with Fleet Street and the City is the **Law Centre** (Royal Courts of Justice, 1874-82), London's last major project in

Gothic-Revival style. The buildings, with over 1000 rooms and four miles of corridor, deal mainly with civil cases; exterior and great hall rich in statuary and other decoration. ▶ The **Victoria Embankment** (the section from Charing Cross Station to Blackfriars), with original decorated seats and lamp standards, is also marked by **Cleopatra's Needle** (erected 1877) and various statues. ▶ In the **Embankment Gardens** is York Watergate (1626), marking the old river bank. ▶ Just E is the Adelphi Terrace, the work of Robert Adam and his brothers. Nearby John Adam Street and Adam Street still have period houses. ▶ The **Sherlock Holmes** pub, Northumberland Avenue, has decor inspired by its subject.   □

▶ SYON PARK AND HOUSE**

map p. 96-A1-2/British Rail: Syon Lane.

Syon Park, Brentford, faces Kew Gardens (→) across the Thames. Syon House, on the site of a monastery, dates from the 16thC and has a dramatic, sometimes gruesome, past, involving Henry VIII among others. It was largely restyled in the 18thC by Robert Adam, while Lancelot Capability Brown landscaped the park.

▶ The W front of the house, castellated but unadorned, gives no hint of the rich interior : **Red Drawing Room**, with crimson silk walls, has Stuart portraits of royalty by Van Dyck and others; **State Dining Room**, Classically styled with niches, half domes, mirrors, friezes and copies of antique statuary; **Long Gallery**, 136 ft. long, only 14 ft. wide, cleverly designed by Adam to compensate for these proportions. Park includes the **Great Conservatory** (1827) and a **rose garden**; Gardening Centre (*Good Fri.-Oct.: Sun.-Thu., 12-5; Oct.: Sun. only, 12-5*).   □

▶ TATE GALLERY*

map 11-E5/Millbank. Underground: Pimlico. Bus: 2, 36, 88, 185.

Built on the site of Millbank Prison, financed by sugar producer Sir Henry Tate and opened 1897, the gallery specializes in British and modern art with many changing exhibitions. The biggest event since its inception was the opening of the Clore Gallery, 1987, a whole new wing eventually bringing together all the works of the Turner Bequest — nearly 300 oil paintings and 19,000 watercolours and drawings.

▶ To the left of the main entrance hall are galleries (2-23) devoted to British art of various periods — Blake, Constable, the pre-Raphaelites, Whistler, Sickert. ▶ To the right of the main entrance are the galleries (30-39) presenting Impressionist, post-Impressionist, Fauvist, Cubist, Surrealist and other recent schools — Monet, Van Gogh, Gauguin, Cezanne, Seurat, Degas, Matisse, Derain, Picasso, Braque, Klee, Max Ernst, Dali, Magritte, Mirò, Mondrian, Chagall. ▶ The large central galleries (27, 29) are usually reserved for special exhibitions; other galleries display paintings and sculpture by Bacon, Hockney, Henry Moore, Barbara Hepworth and many other British and foreign 20thC artists (*Mon.-Sat., 10-5.50, Sun., 2-5.50; Cl. I Jan., Good Fri., May Day, 24-26 Dec.*).   □

▶ TEMPLE**

map 6-F3/Underground: Temple. Bus: 6, 9, 11, 15.

Situated at the W limit of the City (→), between Fleet Street and the Thames (with access from Fleet Street and Victoria Embankment), the area of the Temple takes its name from the Knights Templar, the medieval para-military order, who owned the land until the 14thC. It then became the domain of lawyers, and has remained so, forming the Inner and Middle Temple, two of the Inns of Court.

▶ **Temple Church** (*Apr.-Oct.: 10-5 daily; Nov.-Mar.: 10-4.30; open for services only Christmas Day; Cl. 26 Dec.*), built by the Templars, dates from the 12thC, with 19th and 20thC restoration. A blend of Norman and Gothic styles, with a rare circular nave, modeled either on the Church of the Holy Sepulchre or the Dome of the Rock, Jerusalem. Inside are stone effigies of Templar knights, a tiny penitential cell, fine 17thC carved reredos and windows bearing the crests of the Inner and Middle Temples.
▶ **Middle Temple Hall** (*14th - 16thC; Mon.-Fri., 10-12, 3-4.30, Sat., 10-4; Cl. Sun. and Bank Hols.*) has an oak double hammer-beam roof and Tudor furnishings, plus royal portraits and suits of armour and is rich in history.
▶ **King's Bench Walk** (Inner Temple) has terraces built mainly to designs by Wren; playwright Oliver Goldsmith lived at no. 3. ▶ **Inner and Middle Temple** gardens extend to the Victoria Embankment.   □

▶ THE THAMES*

Though small by world standards, the Thames (Roman *Tamesis*) broadens into an estuary through London, being at one time much wider at certain points than it is today. This gives rise to the strong tides, with big variations between high and low water marks. The Thames has been central to London's history, allowing it to prosper as a major seaport until well into this century, when ships became too big for most of its docks and handling facilities. Several of its local tributaries, notably the Fleet (no longer visible), have also played a big part in the city's history and development. From the 12th to the 19thC, control of the Thames was largely in the hands of the City of London. Then came the Thames Conservancy Board, the Port of London Authority and, since 1974, the Thames Water Authority, marking the change from commerce and industry to water conservation and environmental improvement (*regular riverboat services Easter-Sep. from Westminster and Charing Cross Piers, to points downstream as far as Greenwich, and upstream to Hampton Court*).

▶ **Teddington Lock** (1912) marks the river's tidal limit upstream. ▶ Moored by the **Embankment**, between Waterloo and Blackfriars bridges (→Thames Bridges), are two WWI naval sloops, *Wellington* and *Chrysanthemum*, and a WWII frigate, *President.* ▶ Moored by Tower Bridge (→Thames Bridges) is **HMS Belfast** (*access by ferry from Tower Pier or Symon's Wharf, Tooley Street Daily: 11-5.50; Nov.-Mar.: 11-4.30; Cl. 1 Jan., Good Fri., May Day, 24-26 Dec.*), WWII cruiser, a free extension of the Imperial War Museum (→). ▶ **St. Katherine's Dock**, just beyond Tower Bridge, now restored as a marina and museum of historic river and coastal craft. ▶ The 16thC **'Prospect of Whitby'**, at Wapping, is London's best-known riverside pub, frequented by Pepys, Dickens and other celebrities. ▶ Nearby is Execution Dock, where pirates were hanged up to the beginning of the 19thC.
▶ The **Thames Barrier** (1982) at Woolwich, spanning over 500 yards from bank to bank, is the river's greatest engineering achievement; designed to protect London from flooding by the growing risk of high tides, it has four main steel gates (each weighing 3000 tons), and six smaller ones: when opened — lowered into the water — ships pass over them.   □

▶ THAMES BRIDGES*

From Roman times until the 18thC, London was served by a single bridge over the Thames. Longest standing was the 12thC London Bridge, cluttered with tall
houses and a chapel, and constantly menaced by fire
and flood, but which survived until the early 19thC.
Today thirty-one bridges — road, rail and pedestrian
— span the river from Hampton Court upstream, to
Tower Bridge.

▶ **Richmond** (1774), a toll bridge well into the 19thC, since
widened but retaining its rural character. ▶ Beyond the
railway and Twickenham bridges is Richmond footbridge
(1890), forming part of lock and sluice gates controlling
the tidal flow. ▶ **Hammersmith** (1887), an exuberant Victorian suspension bridge, replacing an earlier one of similar
construction. ▶ **Albert** (1873), another decorative suspension bridge. ▶ **Westminster** (1862), replacing the bridge of
1750 that inspired Wordsworth's famous sonnet. ▶ **Hungerford** (1864), best-known of London's railway bridges,
also a footbridge; it features in several of Monet's Impressionist paintings of London. ▶ **Waterloo** (1939), biggest
of London's bridges, poised high above the river and the
Embankment, with a fine view of St. Paul's (→) and the
City (→) skyline. ▶ **Blackfriars** (1869), solidly Victorian, of
iron and stone. Next to it are the massive cast-iron stan-
chions of the old railway bridge. ▶ **London** (1973), newest
of all the bridges, replacing that of 1831 which, in turn,
had replaced the 12thC bridge; the 1831 bridge has been
re-erected at Lake Havasu City, Arizona, U.S.A. ▶ **Tower
Bridge** (1894), the last before the sea, and one of London's most celebrated landmarks. It is a double bascule
or drawbridge, designed to allow shipping into the old
Pool of London. The twin Gothic-Revival towers house
the bridge machinery and also lifts that originally con-
veyed pedestrians to a high-level footbridge, since the
main bridge was often raised several times a day, now
the raising of the bridge is something of an event.   □

▶ TOWER OF LONDON***

map 7-H3/Tower Hill. Underground: Tower Hill. Bus: 15.

The fortress was begun by William the Conqueror
soon after the Norman Conquest (1066), both as
a symbol·of his authority and as a defense against
attack from the river. It was added to over the centuries by a succession of monarchs, and used as a
royal residence, prison and place of execution (the
last prisoner was Rudolf Hess in WWII), treasury and
jewel house, mint, armoury, and menagerie. It is now
a museum of priceless relics, attended by the Yeomen Warders ('Beefeaters'), originally a royal body-
guard in Tudor uniform. Riverside guns fire salutes on
State occasions.

▶ **White Tower** or Keep (1077-97) was the original fortress. It was whitewashed in 1241, hence its name, and
the turret cupolas were added in the 14thC. It houses the
Royal Armoury, one of the greatest collections of arms
and armour. **St. John's Chapel** is a fine example of Norman church architecture. ▶ **The Crown Jewels** (Jewel
House) date from the Restoration, most earlier royal rega-
lia having been sold or melted down by Cromwell. They
include the **Imperial State Crown**, with 3000 jewels, and
the **Royal Sceptre**, containing the Star of Africa, the
world's biggest diamond. Also swords of state and other
treasures. ▶ **Bloody Tower** (12thC), where Sir Walter
Raleigh was incarcerated for 12 years prior to his execution. ▶ **Traitor's Gate** and **St. Thomas's Tower** (14thC),
the main entrance from the river, leading to the **Wake-
field Tower**. ▶ **Royal Fusiliers Museum, New Armouries**
and **Waterloo Barracks** containing arms and other rega-
lia of the regiment, also the Oriental Gallery of arms and

armour from India, Burma, China and Japan. ▶ **Tower Green** was an execution and burial place, numbering among its victims Anne Boleyn and Catherine Howard. (Many more were executed on neighbouring Tower Hill.) The moat was drained and grassed over in the 19thC. ▶ The Yeomen Warders parade each day at 11 a.m., and perform the Ceremony of the Keys each evening at 10 p.m.; (*admission on application only*). ▶ A special feature is the ravens (→; *Mar.-Oct.: Mon.-Sat., 9.30-5.45; Nov.-Feb.: Mon.-Sat., 9.30-4.30.*).   □

Tower of London

The building of Europe's oldest fortress prison was started in the 11thC by William the Conqueror and, in the course of its gory history, it has served as a palace, prison, armoury, and again as a prison during the 20thC world wars. As a royal fortress and state prison it has witnessed many executions, scenes of torture and long periods of incarceration. Many famous people, including Henry VIII's second wife, Anne Boleyn, Thomas More and Lady Jane Grey, have lost their heads here, and Sir Walter Raleigh was imprisoned three times in the Tower — once for twelve years. The last man to be beheaded was Lord Lovat in 1747; but spies during both world wars were shot here and Rudolf Hess was imprisoned at the Tower in 1941.

Walls in the fortress have been inscribed by numerous unfortunate inmates: the name 'Jane' can be seen in two places in the Beauchamp Tower where Lady Jane Grey's young husband, Lord Dudley, was imprisoned before his execution. There are also said to be ghosts. In the White Tower noises of people groaning under torture have been heard, and the headless figure of Anne Boleyn, dressed in white, appears on Tower Green where royalty and nobles were beheaded (commoners met their death outside on Tower Hill). On moonlit nights Walter Raleigh patrols Raleigh's Walk — but if disturbed will instantly disappear. Tower Green is still inhabited by the ominous black ravens, and it is believed that if these leave, the Tower will fall and England will be doomed. About forty Yeoman Warders, dressed in Tudor costume, guard the Tower; every night at half past nine the Chief Warden locks the gates and hands the keys to the Resident Governor — as he has done for the past 700 years.

▶ TWICKENHAM*

map p. 96-A2/British Rail: St. Margaret, Twickenham, Strawberry Hill, Whitton.

For sportsmen, Twickenham means the international rugby football ground. But this large W London suburb across the Thames from Richmond (→) also has a history and places of notable architectural merit and interest.

▶ **Marble Hill House** (1728; *Mon.-Thu., Sat., Sun., 10-5; Nov.-Jan.: 10-4; Cl. 24-26 Dec.*), a splendid Classical-Revival (Palladian) villa in its own grounds, built by Henrietta Howard, mistress of George II, and frequented by her friend, the poet Alexander Pope; interior and furnishings have been restored as closely as possible to the original.▶ Next to it, in a riverside garden, **Orleans House Gallery** (*Apr.-Sep.: Tue.-Sat., 1-5.30, Sun., Bank Hols., 2-5.30; Oct.-Mar.: Tue.-Sat.,1-4.30, Sun., Bank Hols., 2-4.30*), the remaining wing of a large 18thC mansion, once the home of the exiled French Duke of Orléans, later King Louis-Philippe. The gallery shows temporary exhibitions. ▶ Between Marble Hill and Orleans House is **Montpellier Row**, a fine Georgian terrace (1722). ▶ The parish church of **St. Mary the Virgin**; mainly Georgian with medieval tower, has a handsome interior: memorial to Alexander Pope, who is buried here. ▶ **Strawberry Hill** (1776), built by Horace Walpole, son of Prime Minister Sir Robert Walpole and man of letters, in early Gothic-Revival style, with a most fanciful interior; now a theological college (*conducted tours Wed., Sat. on application*). ▶ **Kneller Hall**, built 1711 by court artist Sir Godfrey Kneller, but largely rebuilt 1848 in Neojacobean style; home of the Royal Military School of Music.   □

▶ VICTORIA AND ALBERT MUSEUM*

map 8-B4/Cromwell Road. Underground: South Kensington. Bus: 14, 30, 74.

The museum, founded 1857 in the wake of the Great Exhibition of 1851 and named after Queen Victoria and her consort, is devoted to fine and applied arts of all countries, styles and periods. The huge collection did not acquire its present home until 1909. The massive building by Sir Aston Webb is surmounted by a tower in the form of an imperial crown.

▶ Lower ground floor: Boiler House project, exhibitions of history, theory and practice of design and consumer products. ▶ Ground floor: Raphael cartoons; dress collection; Indian, Islamic and oriental art; early medieval art and tapestries; Gothic art; Renaissance art; Henry Cole wing of prints, drawings, photographs and paintings; English Renaissance and British art. ▶ First floor: musical instruments; English and continental ironwork; 20thC British art and design; English and continental silver; jewelry; British and continental church plate; tapestries, carpets, lace, embroidery, textiles; stained glass; British art. ▶ Second floor : pottery, ceramics, enamels (*Mon.-Thu., Sat., 10-5.30, Sun., 2.30-5.30; Cl. 1 Jan., Good Fri., May Day, 24-26 Dec.*).   □

▶ VICTORIA AND PIMLICO*

map 10-D4/Underground: Victoria, Pimlico. Bus: 11, 24, 25, 29.

The low-lying area contained by the bend in the river S of Westminster (→) and Buckingham Palace (→) remained largely neglected until the 19thC. Then the creation of new streets, the extension of Thomas Cubitt's Knightsbridge and Belgravia (→) development, and the building of Victoria Station (→Railway Stations) brought intensive housing and commerce to the two neighbouring districts. Victoria remains largely commercial, while Pimlico is characterized by Victorian terraces and squares.

▶ **Victoria Street**, running from Victoria Station to Parliament Square, is one of London's busiest, with the Victoria Palace variety theatre, the new Army and Navy Stores (rebuilt 1977 as the Army and Navy Victoria), and New Scotland Yard (1967), headquarters of London Metropolitan Police. ▶ Separated from Victoria Street by a small piazza is the Neobyzantine Roman Catholic **Westminster Cathedral** (John Francis Bentley, 1895-1903); the most striking external feature is the 280-ft. domed bell tower or campanile; the building is also exceptionally long (360 ft.), with the widest nave in England. The rich interior decor of marble and mosaics, though impressive, is only half finished: the Stations of the Cross are by designer and sculptor Eric Gill; a giant Rood or Crucifix hangs from the main arch of the nave. ▶ Just S of Victoria Street, in

Greycoat Place, is the restored **Greycoat School** (1701), in Queen Anne style, with wooden figures of a boy and girl in old charity school uniforms. ▶ The surviving building of the **Bluecoat School** (1709), N of Victoria Street, in Caxton Street, is the memorial to another charity school, with the statue of a pupil in blue coat above the door. ▶ Millbank riverfront is marked by the 387-ft. **Millbank Tower** (1963) and the **Tate Gallery** (→).   [ ]

▶ WALLACE COLLECTION*

map 4-C3/Hertford House, Manchester Square. Underground: Bond Street. Bus: 6, 7, 12, 15, 30, 73, 74, 88, 159.

Hertford House (1777, enlarged 1882), on the N side of Manchester Square, is the home of this major collection of fine art, furnishings, arms and armour, brought together by members of the Hertford family, including Sir Richard Wallace, whose widow bequeathed it to the nation in 1900.

▶ Paintings by Holbein, Titian, Canaletto, Rubens, Rembrandt, Frans Hals (*The Laughing Cavalier*), Velasquez (*Lady with a Fan*), Poussin (*Dance to the Music of Time*), Fragonard (*The Swing*), Watteau, Reynolds, Gainsborough, Lawrence; Sèvres porcelain; Venetian glass; Limoges enamels; 17th and 18thC French furniture and clocks, including pieces for Louis XV and Marie-Antoinette; Renaissance gold and silver work; Medieval to 18thC European arms and armour, also oriental pieces. [ ]

▶ WEMBLEY STADIUM AND CONFERENCE CENTRE*

map p. 96-A1/Underground, British Rail: Wembley Central.

The 13-acre stadium in NW London, built for the British Empire Exhibition of 1923, has since been Britain's premier venue for national and international sporting events, including the 1948 Olympic Games and 1966 World Cup Soccer Football Final. Around it have gathered other major sporting and entertainments facilities, and, most recently, a Conference Centre.

▶ The Wembley Stadium Tour (*10, 11, 12, 2, 5, also 4 in the summer, Thu., Christmas and days of big events*) takes visitors round the 100,000-capacity stadium, including the dressing rooms, famous Player's Tunnel and Royal Box. ▶ **Wembley Arena** (formerly 1934 Empire Pool) stages ice shows, ice hockey, boxing, gymnastics and many other sporting events, also pop concerts. ▶ The **International Conference Centre** (1977), with large auditorium also used as a concert hall.   [ ]

▶ WESTMINSTER*

map 10-E4/Underground: Westminster. Bus: 3, 11, 12, 24, 25, 29, 53, 88, 159.

The modern City of Westminster is a large administrative area. The district, centred round the site of the old Palace of Westminster and Westminster Abbey (→), is one of the oldest parts of London outside the City (→) itself. Despite the palace and abbey, it was quite a disreputable area up to the 19thC, when the present Houses of Parliament (→) were built and adjacent Parliament Square laid out, giving it today's dignified atmosphere.

▶ At the corner of Westminster Bridge and Victoria Embankment is the bronze **statue** of Queen Boudicca and daughters in a war chariot (1855). ▶ By the **Embankment** is the imposing **Norman Shaw Building** (1906), named after its architect, formerly New Scotland Yard and head-quarters of London's Metropolitan Police. ▶ **Parliament Square** (1868), bordered by the Houses of Parliament and Westminster Abbey, has statues to British Prime Ministers Lord Palmerston, Canning, Peel, Disraeli and Sir Winston Churchill (1973), also to President Lincoln and Field Marshal Smuts (Epstein, 1958). ▶ In the shadow of Westminster Abbey is **St. Margaret's**, parish church of the House of Commons dating from the 15thC, with 19thC restorations by Sir Giles Gilbert Scott; it has Tudor monuments and some fine stained glass; Samuel Pepys, John Milton, Sir Walter Raleigh and Admiral Blake are buried here. ▶ W of Parliament Square is the large **Methodist Central Hall** (1905), used for public gatherings, and the new Conference Centre (1985). ▶ The corner of Victoria Street and Great Smith Street marks the site of William Caxton's first British **printing press** (1476). ▶ Just behind, approached through a gateway from Broad Sanctuary, is **Dean's Yard**, with **Church House**, used during WWII by both houses of parliament, **Westminster Abbey Choir School**, and, through another gateway, historic **Westminster School**. ▶ A few minutes' walk away is **Smith Square** (1726), with national headquarters of the Conservative and Labour (Transport House) parties. In the middle of the square is the Baroque **St. John's Church** (Thomas Archer, 1714), restored after WWII bombing and now a public hall, much used for concerts.   ⌷

▶ **WESTMINSTER ABBEY***

map 11-E4/Underground: Westminster. Bus: 3, 11, 12, 24, 25, 29, 53, 88, 159.

Edward the Confessor's abbey of 1042-66 was largely replaced by Henry III, whose 13thC Gothic edifice represents the bulk of the present abbey, with two major additions in the shape of Henry VII's Chapel (1503) and Nicholas Hawksmoor's twin W towers (1735). It has seen the coronation of every English or British monarch since William I in 1066. Many of the nation's most famous men and women are either buried within its precincts or are commemorated there.

▶ Facing the W entrance, in the centre of the nave, is the **Tomb of the Unknown Soldier**, commemorating the dead of WWI. Next to it is a commemorative **plaque** to Sir Winston Churchill and nearby, another to President Roosevelt. ▶ The **nave** is noted for its Gothic vaulting; organ, choir stalls and screen are 18th and 19thC respectively. ▶ Beyond the choir and Sanctuary is **Edward the Confessor's Chapel**, containing Edward's shrine and the tombs of eight other kings and queens. ▶ This chapel also houses the 13thC oak **Coronation Chair** with, beneath it, the **Stone of Scone** (ancient Scottish coronation stone taken by Edward I). It has been used for every coronation since 1308, for which ceremonies it is moved round the 15thC stone screen, to face the Sanctuary. ▶ Beyond Edward the Confessor's Chapel is that of Henry VII, with magnificent Perpendicular fan **vaulting**, and the tombs of Henry VII himself, Elizabeth I, Mary Queen of Scots and other royal personages. ▶ The **Battle of Britain Chapel** at the far end (founded 1947) includes the tombs of RAF leaders Lords Trenchard and Dowding. ▶ **Poet's Corner**, in the S transept, has the tombs of Chaucer, Jonson (buried upright), Dryden, Johnson, Sheridan, Browning, Tennyson and memorials to Shakespeare, Blake, Milton, Keats, Shelley, Byron, Wordsworth, Dickens, Hardy, Kipling and, alone among composers, Handel. ▶ Others buried in the abbey or commemorated are, among scientists and inventors, Michael Faraday, Lords Rutherford and Lister, Robert Stephenson, James Watt; and Prime Ministers Pitt the Elder and Younger, Palmerston, Disraeli, Gladstone, Asquith, Lloyd George, Attlee. ▶ The 13thC **Chapter House** has Gothic vaulting, fine tiled floor and 13th and 14thC sculptures and paintings. ▶ The 13th and14thC **cloisters** have a brass rubbing centre. ▶ The abbey **museum** (*separate entrance and admission charge*) has wooden or wax funeral effigies of several monarchs, Henry V's shield and helmet from Agincourt and other treasures (*nave and cloisters open weekdays 8-6, Wed., 8-7.45; other parts of the abbey: Mon.-Fri., 9-4.45, Sat., 9-2.45, 3.45-5.45; Sun. open to visitors between services*).

▶ WHITECHAPEL*

map 7-H3/Underground: Aldgate East, Whitechapel.

Bordering the City (→) to the E, Whitechapel was once noted for coaching inns and markets by the main road from the E coast, and for heavy industries serving the City and nearby docks. Poverty and overcrowding were at their worst in the 19thC, with a large, mainly Jewish immigrant population; notoriety was added by the murders of Jack the Ripper. It remains a place of bustling local industry and commerce, a vital part of London's East End.

▶ **Whitechapel Art Gallery** 1897 (*Tue.-Sun., 11-5.50, Tue., Thu., 11-7.50*), a striking building in Art Nouveau style, has changing exhibitions through the year, mainly of modern art. ▶ **Petticoat Lane** (Middlesex Street): Sunday market is the most famous of all London's street markets (→ Markets). ▶ **Whitechapel Bell Foundry**, founded 1420, a distinguished survivor of the district's old industries; among the bells cast were those for Westminster Abbey (→) and Big Ben (→ Houses of Parliament). ▶ **Trinity Almshouses** (1695), Mile End Road, originally built for retired seamen or their widows, with a handsome chapel at one end. ▶ **St. George-in-the-East** (Hawksmoor, 1714), an imposing church in English Renaissance style, bombed in WWII but restored, with windows by Sir Joshua Reynolds.

▶ WHITEHALL*

map 11-E4/Underground: Westminster, Charing Cross. Bus: 3, 11, 12, 24, 25, 29, 53, 88, 159.

The thoroughfare of Whitehall, running from Trafalgar Square to Parliament Square, takes its name from the former royal palace, burned down in 1698. Soon after, Whitehall itself was widened and flanked by the ministeries and other major government offices that have shaped its character to the present time.

▶ **Trafalgar Square** was planned by Nash and modeled by Sir Charles Barry, 1840. With the National Gallery (→) on its N side, its most famous feature is **Nelson's Column** (1839), the 17-ft. figure of the admiral being added four years later; the bronze reliefs round its base, cast from captured cannon, celebrate his victories. The **lions** are by Landseer. There are other statues in the square to George IV and General Napier and, just to the S, facing Whitehall, an equestrian statue of Charles I. ▶ The Palladian-style **Horse Guards** building (William Kent, 1745) is presided over by sentries of the Horse Guards cavalry regiments, who parade each day (*11a.m., 10a.m., Sun., 4p.m.*). On the far side is **Horse Guards Parade**, flanked to the N by the **Admiralty Building**, and to the S by the rear of Downing Street, where the Trooping of the Colour ceremony takes place each June. There are **statues** to Field Marshals Kitchener, Wolseley and Roberts, and the **Cadiz Memorial**, a huge French mortar mounted on a cast-iron dragon, captured during the Peninsular War (1812). ▶ Opposite the Horse Guards, in Whitehall, is the Renaissance-style **Banqueting House** (*Tue.-Sat., 10-5.30, Sun., 2-5.30; Cl. I Jan., Good Fri., 24-26 Dec., Bank Hols.*), built by Inigo Jones, 1619, for James I, and the only surviving part of Whitehall Palace. Charles I commissioned the painted **ceiling** by Rubens, and was executed outside in 1649. ▶ **No. 10 Downing Street** has been the official home of prime ministers since 1731; the Cabinet regularly meets here. **No. 11** is the home of the chancellor of the exchequer. ▶ At the far end of King Charles Street (between the buildings of the Foreign and Home offices) are the WWII underground **Cabinet War Rooms** (*Tue.-Sun., 10-5.50; Cl. I Jan., Good Fri., May Day, 24-26 Dec., Mon.*), preserved exactly as they were when used by Churchill and his war-time government. ▶ Back in Whitehall stands the **Cenotaph** (Sir Edwin Lutyens, 1919), a national memorial to the dead of two World Wars, and focal point for an annual service of Remembrance on the nearest Sunday to WWI Armistice Day (*II Nov.026*). ▶ Nearby are **statues** to Field Marshals Earl Haig and Viscount Montgomery of Alamein.

□

▶ WIMBLEDON*

map p. 96-A2/Underground, British Rail: Wimbledon.

This South London district has a long history, centred round the High Street at the top of Wimbledon Hill, though little of historical interest remains. Its great fame comes from its international tennis championships, while its attraction for many Londoners is the Common, one of the capital's largest open spaces.

▶ The **All England Lawn Tennis and Croquet Club** was founded 1869, and its annual tennis championships are a world sporting event. The associated **Lawn Tennis Museum** (*Tue.-Sat., 11-5, Sun.,2-5; Cl. Mon., Bank Hols; open only to spectators during the championship fortnight in June*) has many historical relics of the game. ▶ **Wimbledon Common**, over 1000 acres of largely natural heathland, includes a **Wind Flour Mill** (1817), handsomely restored, with a small museum of agricultural relics.

□

Frost fairs

A number of exceptionally severe winters have had a memorable effect on London's River Thames. On several recorded occasions, part of the river has frozen solid and Londoners have taken advantage of this to turn it into a sort of pleasure ground. During the winter of 1564, the Thames was more crowded with people than any street in the city, and lively games of football took place there. In 1684, the diarist John Evelyn recorded how all sorts of booths were arranged in 'streets' upon the ice, and visitors (including King Charles II) could have their names printed on special cards by an enterprising entrepreneur who had set up a press there. During the winter of 1715-16, the river was thickly frozen for a distance of several miles, and entertainments to be enjoyed included the roasting of a whole ox on the ice. For weeks, in Jan. 1740, people lived in temporary 'towns' on the frozen water; while at the 'frost fair' of 1814, a sheep was cooked and sold in slices as 'Lapland mutton'. On this occasion there were musicians to accompany dancing, merry-go-rounds and skittle games. The ice, which was solid between London and Blackfriars bridges, lasted for nearly a week; unfortunately the thaw, when it came, was sudden. Some of the traders, reluctant to lose customers, stayed longer than was wise; three people were drowned, vast numbers got soaked, and a strange assortment of tents, merry-go-rounds and printing presses could be seen stranded on blocks of ice which floated down the river. In 1832, old London Bridge, with its narrow arches, was replaced by a new bridge which allowed the water to flow more freely: the Thames never again froze in the same way.

● Practical information

Ⓘ *London Visitor and Convention Bureau*: 26 Grosvenor Gardens, SW1, ☎ 730 3488, open Mon. to Fri., 9 to 5.30, written and telephone inquiries only. *London Tourist Information Centre*, Victoria Station Forecourt, SW1, open daily, 9 to 8.30, till 10 Jul. and Aug. (bookshop closes at 8, book for guided tours before 7.30). *Selfridges Department Store* (ground floor), Oxford Street, W1, open 9 to 6 Mon. to Sat. except Thu., 9 to 7.30. *Harrods Department Store* (fourth floor), Brompton Road, SW1, open 9 to 5, Mon. to Fri., 9.30 to 5, Wed., 9 to 6, Sat. *Heathrow Central Underground Station*, open daily 9 to 6. *Tower of London* (west gate), EC3, open 10 to 6, Mon. to Sat., 10.15 to 6, Sun. *Piccadilly Circus Underground Station*, multilingual information staff, bookshop, direct no-fee ticket booking for Royal Festival Hall, open 10 to 8 daily.

Embassies and consulates: *American Embassy*, 24 Grosvenor Square, W1, ☎ 499 9000; *French Embassy*, 58 Knightsbridge, SW1, ☎ 235 8080; *Canadian High Commission*, Mcdonald House, 38 Grosvenor Street, W1, ☎ 629 9492; *Irish Embassy*, 17 Grosvenor Place, SW1, ☎ 235 2171.

Further information: the most detailed sources of information for the visitor are the weeklies *Time Out*, *City Limits* and *What's On in London*, which come out on Wed. and are sold at all newsagents and newsstands. These publications provide full information on theatres, shows, cinemas, concerts, exhibitions, festivals, TV, radio, children's activities, etc., along with practical information compiled for Londoners as much as for visitors.

Emergency: medical emergency treatment is free. Dial 999 and ask for an ambulance. *Capital Helpline*, ☎ 388 7575, is open Mon. to Fri. 9.30 to 5.30 to direct callers to specialists who can help with their problem. *The Samaritans*, St. Stephen's, 39 Walbrook Road, EC4, ☎ 283 3400, open 24 hours a day to the depressed and suicidal. *Teledate*, ☎ 200 0200, a 24-hour service with details of all emergency services. *Pharmacy: Wayman Freed*, 45 Golders Green Road, NW11, ☎ 455 4351, open 9.30 to midnight daily. *Dental Emergency Care*, ☎ 677 6363/584 1008, 24-hours a day. *Lost Property*: inform local police station. London Transport operates a 24-hour recorded message for lost property, ☎ 486 2496.

Guided tours: *London Transport*, ☎ 222 1234 operates half and full day tours from Wilton Road Coach Station. Advance booking at any London Travel Enquiry office (no phone bookings). Weekly information sheets as mentioned above and local newspapers give details of the numerous independent lecturers and walking tour associations available.

Big Ben

The name 'Big Ben' refers to the largest bell in the chime of the clock on the Houses of Parliament, although the name is used for both the clock and its bell tower by Westminster Bridge, London's most famous landmark. The clock took 15 years to complete and is not only England's largest clock, but also its most accurate. The clock requires winding only once a week, but before automatic winding-gear was installed in 1913 it took two men 32 hours to complete the operation. The familiar chime, the length of which increases at each quarter until it is sounded complete on the hour, is played on four bells which were made and hung in the belfry without problems, but the fifth bell, which strikes the hour, created enormous difficulties. The first bell made cracked during trials, and the second cracked after it had been put in place, though it was repaired. The name itself remains something of a mystery, but it seems to have been coined by The Times, who announced that 'Big Ben has cracked' in October 1857, playing also upon the news of the retirement, after a 60-round fight, of the boxer Benjamin Caunt.

Post office: *Central Post Office*, Trafalgar Square, 24 William IV Street, WC2, ☎ 930 9580.

Banks: open daily except Sat., Sun. and bank holidays. Principal clearing banks (National Westminster, Midland, Barclays, Lloyds) have foreign departments that cash travelers checks during banking hours: 9.30 to 3.30 Mon. to Fri. Certain branches are open 9.30 to noon or 12.30 Sat.

Foreign exchange offices: the following exchange bureaux are open 24 hours a day, 7 days a week: *Chequepoint*, 548 Oxford Street, W1, ☎ 723 2646; *Erskine*, 15 Shaftesbury Avenue, W1, ☎ 734 1400; *Lenlyn*, Victoria British Rail Station, SW1, ☎ 828 8367; Heathrow and Gatwick airports both have 24-hour banks. *American Express*, 6 Haymarket, SW1, ☎ 930 4411; *Thomas Cook*, 45 Berkeley Street, W1, ☎ 499 4000.

British Rail: *British Rail Travel Centre* (24 hours, multilingual): 12 Lower Regent Street, SW1. Open 9 to 6.30, Mon. to Sat., 10 to 4 Sun. Charing Cross, ☎ 928 5100; Euston, ☎ 387 7070; Holborn Viaduct, ☎ 928 5100; King's Cross, ☎ 278 2477; Liverpool Street, ☎ 283 7171; London Bridge, ☎ 928 5100; Marylebone, ☎ 387 7070; Paddington, ☎ 262 6767; Victoria, ☎ 928 5100; Waterloo, ☎ 928 5100. *Intercity general inquiries*: ☎ 834 2345. For all the above, a central stacking system insures that all phone calls are answered in strict rotation, so be patient and wait for a reply.

Airports: *London Heathrow*, 15 m W, ☎ 759 4321; *British Airways* information, ticket sales and bookings, ☎ 370 5411; access: terminal of Piccadilly Underground line (stop one before the last for Terminal 4, last stop for Terminals 1, 2 and 3). 45 min. tube from London centre every 5 min., 20 hours a day. *Airbuses*: two routes to Heathrow, picking up at 13 points throughout the main hotel areas of Central London. *Gatwick*, ☎ 668 4211, 30 min. from Victoria Station by British Rail Gatwick Express (every 15 min., 5.30 a.m.

to 11 p.m., hourly service throughout the night). Combined Gatwick Express/Underground tickets available from any underground station. *London City Airport (Stolport)*, Connaught Road, Silver Town, London E16 2PX, ☎ 474 5555. Access: Silver Town Station.

Underground (tube): London Regional Transport controls both *red* buses and underground trains. ☎ 222 1234 for their 24 hour a day travel information service (English only). The first trains run from 6 or 6.30 (later on Sun.), and the last at approximately midnight. Under 14 years old reduced fares, and 14 and 15 years old reduced fares with a child-rate photocard (available from post offices in London area). Under 5's travel free. Free maps of tube and bus services and a huge number of ever-changing leaflets describing various fares and special passes are available from underground and bus stations.

Bus service: controlled by London Regional Transport. The map of the city bus network is posted on tube station platforms, bus shelters and main bus stations. Individual bus routes are detailed at bus shelters. Fares on both tube and bus are computed according to stages and zones, therefore a short bus ride crossing three fare zones will cost the same or more than a much longer ride in a single zone. *Tourist pass:* The *Capitalcard* costs £2.50 (£1.25 if under 16) and offers unlimited off-peak travel (i.e., after 9.30 Mon. to Fri.) for the day throughout London by train, underground or bus. Available from British Rail and underground stations. **London By Bus**: book for escorted coach tours of London sights at any London Regional Transport station or at selected travel agents.

Taxis: London black cabs are rated the best in the world. Any cab with its yellow 'for hire' sign lit should stop if you flag it, and provided your journey is under six miles and within the London borders, the cab must take you where you want to go. *Radio Taxis*, ☎ 272 0272/272 3030/253 5000, 24 hours a day. *Minicabs: Addison Lee*, ☎ 720 2161; *Abbey Car Hire*, ☎ 727 2637. Many others listed in yellow pages.

Driving in London: do not use your car in London unless it is absolutely necessary; traffic is extremely dense, with numerous traffic jams. Parking places must nearly always be paid for, either at parking meters or at one of the National Car Parks throughout the city. *Cavendish Square*, ☎ 629 6968; *Piccadilly Circus*, Brewer Street, W1, ☎ 734 9497. For cheaper parking, the *NCP* at the National Theatre, Southbank, SE1, ☎ 928 3940. Free list of locations from NCP, 21 Bryanston Street, W1, ☎ 499 7050. The north and south circular ringroads of London are easily accessible from the centre and link up to all major motorways around London.

Car-rental: *Budget*: Central bookings, ☎ 935 3518; British Rail King's Cross, ☎ 833 0972; NCP car park, Victoria, Semley Place, SW1, ☎ 730 5233. *Avis*: 68 North Row, W1, ☎ 848 8733; Gatwick Airport, ☎ 0293 29721; Heathrow Airport, Hounslow, Middlesex, ☎ 897 9321. *Godfrey Davis Rail Drive* : Kings Cross, ☎ 834 8484; Paddington, ☎ 262 5655; Heathrow Airport, ☎ 897 0811. *Hertz*: Heathrow Airport, ☎ 897 9849; 1272, London Road, ☎ 679 1799.

Excursions on the Thames: upstream: boats leave from Westminster Pier, opposite Big Ben and travel upstream to Kew every 30 min., 10.30 to 3.30. Trips upstream to Hampton Court leave at 10, 10.30, 11.30 and 12, ☎ 930 4721. **Downstream**: boats leave Westminster Pier to the Tower of London (20 min. journey) every 20 min. 10.30 - 4 and to Greenwich (45 min. journey) every 20 min. 10.30 - 4. Three-hour round-trip cruises to the Thames Flood Barrier from Westminster Pier at 10 and 1.30. One-hour cruises every 30 min. 11.30 - 5.

On the Regent Canal: *Zoo Waterbus* departs from Little Venice, Warwick Avenue/Camden Town tubes, ☎ 482 2550; *Jason's Trip* cruise along the canal, Camden Town tube, ☎ 286 3428. Riverboat Information Service, ☎ 730 4812.

Aerial views of London: *UK Air Taxis*, Westland Heliport, Lombard Road, SW11, ☎ 228 9114. Main line station Clapham Junction. *Tempus Aviation*, Grove House, 628 London Road, Colnbrook, Buckinghamshire, ☎ 02812 4750.

Weather forecast: ☎ 836 4311.

Theatre: West End: *Barbican*, EC2, ☎ 628 8795, London home of the Royal Shakespeare Company with plays often directly from Stratford-upon-Avon; *National*, South Bank, SE1, ☎ 928 2252; *Palace*, Shaftesbury Avenue, W1, ☎ 437 8327; *Old Vic*, Waterloo Road, SE1, ☎ 928 7616; *Open Air*, Regent's Park, NW1, ☎ 486 2431; *Drury Lane*, Theatre Royal, Catherine Street, WC2, ☎ 836 8108. **Fringe**: *Albany*, Creek Road, SE8, ☎ 692 0765; *ICA*, Nash House, 12 Carlton House Terrace, SW1, ☎ 930 6393; *Riverside Studios*, Crisp Road, W6, ☎ 748 3354; *Tricycle*, 269 Kilburn High Road, NW6, ☎ 328 8626; *The Little Angel*, marionette theatre for children, 14 Dagmar Passage, Cross Street, N1, ☎ 226 1787. **Theatre ticket agencies**: charge up to 20 % commission but can usually secure tickets advertised as 'sold out' both before and on the same day as a performance: first call ☎ 240 7200, 24 hours a day, for credit card bookings (£1.75 per ticket). *Keith Prowse*, 44 Shaftesbury Avenue, W1, ☎ 437 8976; *SWET Ticket Booth*, southwest corner of Leicester Square, WC2, 2.30-6.30; *Premier Box Office*, 188 Shaftesbury Avenue, W1, ☎ 240 2245/7. Same-day reduced price seats sold at most theatres. Most major hotels also have booking offices in the lobby.

Concert halls: *Barbican Hall*, Barbican Centre, EC2, ☎ 628 8795, 638 8891. *Royal Albert Hall*: Kensington Grove, SW7, ☎ 589 8212, 589 9465. *Royal Festival Hall*, *Queen Elizabeth Hall* and the *Purcell Room* at the South Bank Arts Centre, SE1, ☎ 928 3191, 928 8000. Open-air concerts are given in the summer by the lake at *Crystal Palace*, in Holland Park, Kensington, W8, and at *Kenwood*, Hampstead, N6.

Art galleries: *Barbican*, Barbican Centre for Arts and Conferences, EC2, ☎ 638 4141, for thematic, non-specialized exhibitions; *British Library*, Great Russell Street, WC1, ☎ 636 1544, permanent exhibition of national collection of books and manuscripts, plus temporary exhibitions, lectures and audio-visual programs; *Crafts Council Galleries*, 12 Waterloo Place, SW1, ☎ 930 4811; *Christie's Contemporary Art*, 8 Dover Street, W1, ☎ 499 6701, a commercial gallery with continuous exhibitions by its artists; *Fisher Fine

Art, 30 King Street, St. James, SW1, ☎ 839 3942, exhibitions of 20thC European artists and British realists every 4 to 6 weeks; *Hayward*, Belvedere Road, SE1, ☎ 938 3144, the main platform for the British Arts Council with five interconnected galleries and three sculpture courts; *Institute of Contemporary Arts*, Nash House, 12 Carlton House Terrace, SW1, ☎ 930 0493, platform for all new developments in art, with twenty-four exhibitions annually held in its three galleries; *Marlborough Fine Art*, 6 Albemarle Street, W1, ☎ 629 5161, Impressionist and 20thC art; *National*, Trafalgar Square, WC2, ☎ 839 3321, frequent exhibitions of 'the country's greatest collection of European paintings'; *Royal Academy of Arts*, Piccadilly, W1, ☎ 734 9052, mounts large shows arranged months in advance and extremely popular; *Tate*, Millbank, SW1, ☎ 821 1313, British collection, 1500-1900, modern collection of works by later 19th and 20thC artists; *Waddington*, 2, 4, 31 and 34 Cork Street, W1, ☎ 439 1866, specializing in painting and sculpture; *Anthony d'Offay*, 9 and 23 Dering Street, W1, ☎ 629 1578, a private gallery with 10-12 exhibitions annually of British and international contemporary art.

Antiques: There is a huge amount of 18th and 19thC furniture, china and *objets d'art* available throughout London. By far the best places for hunting are Portobello and Camden Passage markets (→ *markets* below) and the Chelsea Antiques Fair, Chelsea Old Town Hall, Kings Road, SW3, ☎ 937 5464, usually held in Mar. and Sep. Many antique shops also deal in silverware and jewelry, particularly those in the Burlington Arcade, SW1. *Antique shops*: *T. Crowther*, 282 North End Road, SW6, ☎ 385 1375; *Jeremy*, 255 Kings Road, SW3, ☎ 352 0644; *Pelham Galleries*, 163 and 165 Fulham Road, SW3, ☎ 589 2686; *Barrett Street Antique Supermarket*, W1, ☎ 493 5833; *Gray's Antique Market*, Davies Street, W1, over 100 stalls with wide range of antiques; *Chelsea Antique Market*, Kings Road, SW3. *Jewelry and silver*: *Bentley*, 65 New Bond Street, W1, ☎ 629 0651; *Bond Street Silver Galleries*, 111-112 New Bond Street, W1, ☎ 493 6180; *Collingwood*, 46 Conduit Street, W1, ☎ 734 2656; *Garrard*, 112 Regent Street, W1, ☎ 734 7020, jewelers to the Queen; *S.J. Phillips*, 139 New Bond Street, W1, ☎ 629 6261.

Auction rooms: *Christie's (South Kensington) Ltd., Art and Antiques*, 85 Old Brompton Road, SW7, ☎ 581 2231; *Christie's Fine Art*, 8 King Street, SW1, ☎ 839 9060, open Mon. to Fri. 9.30 to 4.45; *Phillips*, 7 Blenheim Street, W1, ☎ 629 6602, open 8.30 to 5, Mon. to Fri., 8.30 to 12, Sat.; *Sotheby's*, 34-35 New Bond Street, W1, ☎ 493 8080 and 19 Motcomb Street, SW1, ☎ 235 4311.

Markets: *Bermondsey*, SE1, antiques and bric-a-brac, Fri. from 5 a.m.; *Berwick Street*, W1, Mon. to Sat. for fruit and vegetables; *Brick Lane*, huge flea market on Sun. morning; *Camden Lock*, NW1, Sat. and Sun. for crafts, antiques, bric-a-brac, second-hand and new clothing; *Camden Passage*, NW1, for expensive antiques: 8-4, Tue., Wed., Sat., 9-5, Thu., Fri.; *Columbia Road*, Shoreditch, E2, Sun. morning for flowers and plants; *Electric Avenue*, Brixton, SW9, Mon., Tue., Thu., Fri., Sat. all day, Wed. (mornings only) for second-hand clothing and Afro-Caribbean foods;

Greenwich Antiques Market, Greenwich High Road, SE10, Sat. and Sun. for antiques; *Kensington Market*, Kensington High Street, W8, Mon. to Sat. for modern and unusual clothing; *Leather Lane*, EC1, Mon. to Fri. for fruits and vegetables, plants, clothing; *London Silver Vaults*, Chancery Lane, WC2, Mon. to Fri. and Sat. mornings for antique and modern silver; *Petticoat Lane*, Middlesex Street, EC1, Sun. mornings for general goods; *Portobello Road*, W11, Mon. to Sat. for general goods, Mon.-Thu. bric-a-brac, Fri.-Sat. flea market, Sat. antiques; *Shepherd's Bush*, W12, Mon. to Wed., Fri. and Sat., Thu. mornings for general goods; *Wembley*, Wembley Stadium Car Park, Middlesex, Sun. mornings for clothing, jewelry, food, bric-a-brac. London's *wholesale* markets are almost institutions in themselves, well worth a visit for the lively atmosphere, the range of fresh poultry, game, flowers and fish on display and the continual bartering. Since they are primarily there to serve retailers, hoteliers and restaurateurs who want fresh produce, the markets begin very early (4 a.m. onwards) and are all closed by midday: *Billingsgate*, North Quay, West India Dock Road, E14, Tue. to Sat., London's principal fish market; *New Covent Garden*, Nine Elms, SW5, Mon. to Fri., Sat. 4 to 9 a.m., London's principal fruit and vegetable market, with flowers on Sat.; *Smithfield*, EC1, Mon. to Fri., for meat, poultry and game; *Spitalfields*, E1, Mon. to Fri., Sat. 4.30 to 9 a.m. for fruit, vegetables and flowers.

Clubs, discothèques: *Stringfellows*: where you can rub shoulders with the rich and famous on Peter Stringfellows' glittering dance floor. First class nouvelle cuisine restaurant. 16/19 Upper St. Martin's Lane, WC2, ☎ 240 5534. *Ronnie Scott's*: to be upstairs at Ronnie Scott's, listening either to the man himself or one of his guest jazz bands, is to have made it. 47 Frith Street, W1, ☎ 439 0747. *The Empire Ballroom*: live disco bands, top UK disc jockeys, a light entertainment show and six bars. Leicester Square, WC2, ☎ 437 1446. *The Hippodrome*: a sophisticated nightclub with a laser floor show. Hippodrome Corner, Leicester Square, WC2, ☎ 437 4311. *Xenon*: lavishly equipped with a cocktail bar and hydraulic stage with waterfalls and fountains. 196 Piccadilly, W1, ☎ 734 9344. *100 Club*: a haven for jazz enthusiasts, attracting such names as Acker Bilk and his Paramount Jazz Band, Ken Colyer's All Star Jazz Men and Max Collie's Rhythm Aces. 100 Oxford Street, W1, ☎ 636 0933.

Riding: *Lilo Blum*, 32 Grosvenor Crescent Mews, SW1, ☎ 235 6846, includes rides in Hyde Park; *Bathurst Riding Stables*, 63 Bathurst Mews, W2, ☎ 723 2813; *Fir Tree Farm*, Woodlands Road, Little Bookham, Leatherhead, Surrey, ☎ Bookham 58712; *Roehampton Gate Riding and Livery Stables*, Priory Lane, SW16, adjacent to Richmond Park, ☎ 876 7089.

Cycling: more and more people are taking to the road on bicycles in London, both for economy and health reasons. *The London Cycling Campaign*, ☎ 928 7220, has been set up to provide cyclists with advice and information, and bicycles are available for rent from the following firms: *Bell Street Bikes*, 73 Bell Street, NW1, ☎ 724 0456; *London Bicycle Company*, 'Rent

A Bike', 41 Floral Street, WC2, ☎ 2403211; *Bicycle Revival*, 17-19 Elizabeth Street, SW1, ☎ 7306716.

Golf: many membership courses will extend guest facilities to members of comparable clubs from overseas. *Brent Valley Golf Course*, Church Road, Hanwell, W7, ☎ 5671287, an 18-hole course in Brent River Park; *Richmond Park*, Roehampton Gate, SW15, ☎ 8763205, two 18-hole parkland courses with advanced booking necessary at weekends; *Royal Mid Surrey*, Old Deer Park, Twickenham Road, Richmond, TW9 2SB, ☎ 9401894, two 18-hole parkland courses open Mon. to Fri. Players must be members of recognized clubs and hold a handicap certificate; *South Herts*, Links Drive, Totteridge, N20, ☎ 4452035, an 18-hole parkland course, open Mon. to Fri. Players must be members of recognized clubs. Municipal courses where it is not necessary to be a member: *Twickenham*, Staines Road, Twickenham, Middlesex, ☎ 9796946, 9 hole; *Royal Epping Forest*, Forest Approach, Station Road, Chingford, Essex, ☎ 5291039, 18 hole; *Home Park*, Hampton Wick, Kingston-upon-Thames, Surrey, ☎ 9776645, 18-hole.

London events: **January**: *International Boat Show; West London Antiques Fair; Holiday on Ice*, Wembley Arena; *Brent Festival of Music and Dance; Benson and Hedges Masters Snooker Tournament.* **February**: *International Food and Drink Exhibition; Crufts Dogs Show; Stratford and East London Music Festival; Chinese New Year*, Soho. **March**: *Chelsea Antiques Fair; London International Opera Festival; British Designer Show; London Photograph Fair; Devizes to Westminster International Canoe Race; Oxford v. Cambridge University Boat Race*, Putney to Mortlake; *International Festival of Country Music; Easter Parade*, Battersea Park; *Daily Mail Ideal Home Exhibition.* **April**: *London Book Fair; London Drinker Beer Festival; Champions All International Gymnastics; Craft Fair; London Marathon; Milk Cup Football Final; FA Vase Final; Easter Parade*, Battersea Park; *London Harness Horse Parade*, Regent Park. **May**: *Rugby League Challenge Cup Final; Historic Commercial Vehicle Run*, Battersea Park to Brighton; *Royal Windsor Horse Trials; FA Cup Final; Chelsea Flower Show; International Contemporary Art Fair, Fine Art and Antiques Fair*, Olympia; *Greenwich Festival; Royal Academy of Arts Summer Exhibition; London Marathon*, Greenwich to Westminster. **June**: *Horse Guards Parade 'Beating the Retreat'; Derby Day Horse Racing at Epsom; Stella Artois Tennis Championships; Grosvenor House Antiques Fair; Trooping the Colour; All England Club Lawn Tennis Championships*, Wimbledon; *Metropolitan Police Horse Show; London to Brighton Bicycle Ride; Putney Show*, Putney Lower Common. **July**: *Festival of the City of London; Berkeley Square Charity Ball; Royal Tournament*, Earl's Court; *Richmond Festival; Henry Wood Promenade Concerts (Proms); Finchley Carnival; Chelsea Village Fair; Swan Upping*, River Thames; *Doggetts Coat and Badge Race*, Tower Bridge to Chelsea. **August**: *West London Antiques Fair; Greater London Horse Show; Greenwich Clipper Weeks; Notting Hill Caribbean Carnival.* **September**: *Chelsea Antiques Fair; Battle of Britain Service; Sunday Times Fun Run*, Hyde Park; *Punch and Judy Festival*, Covent Garden Piazza. **October**: *National Brass*

The Gunpowder Plot

The years following the establishment of the Church of England under Henry VIII saw much conflict between English Protestants and Catholics. During the reign of Henry's daughter Mary Tudor, Catholicism was briefly restored, and over 300 Protestants were put to death. But for most of the next 150 years Catholics were regarded as public enemies and could be severely punished for not attending the Anglican Church. There were a number of Catholic uprisings, including a 1586 conspiracy to murder Elizabeth I and put Catholic Mary Queen of Scots in her place. But the most famous plot of all was the 1605 scheme to blow up the Houses of Parliament.

This was to have taken place on 5 Nov., at the state opening of Parliament, and was intended to kill the king, his ministers and all the members of both Houses of Parliament. The plot was organized by Robert Catesby, but it was Guy Fawkes who was to set off the explosion. The conspirators rented a building next to the House of Lords in Dec. 1604, and began tunneling through the cellars. After eleven months they had reached the vaults of Parliament and managed to store thirty-six barrels of gunpowder. However, the plot was betrayed when an anonymous letter was sent to one of the peers. A search was made, and Guy Fawkes was discovered with his lantern, matches and tinderbox. (The plan had been for him to light the explosive with a slow-burning fuse and then to escape in a boat waiting on the Thames.) Fawkes was arrested and later tortured and executed — along with those other conspirators who had not been killed while attempting to escape. Ever since then, festivities have taken place on 5 Nov. in his name. On Guy Fawkes or Bonfire Night, 'Guys' or effigies of Fawkes are burned on bonfires throughout the country and fireworks are lit. Children prop up Guys they have made in the streets, and beg passers-by for 'a penny for the Guy', and before every annual state opening, the cellars of the Houses of Parliament are searched.

Band Championships; Horse of the Year Show; Chelsea Crafts Fair; Trafalgar Day Parade by Sea Cadets; International Bike Show. **November**: *London to Brighton Veteran Car Run; Kensington Antiques Fair; Caravan Camping Holiday Show, Earl's Court; Lord Mayor's Show; London Craft Fair; Daily Mail International Ski Show; Benson and Hedges Tennis Championships; World Travel Market.* **December**: *Olympia International Showjumping Championships; Christmas Lights and Trees, Oxford Street and Regent Street.*

Accommodation: *London Homes*, P.O. Box 730, London, SW6, 2QN, ☎ 748 4947. *London Homes* has gathered close to 80 addresses for reasonably priced places to stay, all located near underground stations. Prices are less than £10 a night per person, including breakfast. For a longer stay, it is possible to rent an apartment (minimum stay: two weeks) starting at £70 a week.

Room and board with a London resident: *London Homestead Services* has 250 houses in its scheme, each offering home comforts and breakfast. Prices start at £10 per person per night at all properties 20 to 30 min. traveling time from Piccadilly. Minimum stay 3 nights. 154 Warwick Road, Kensington, W14, 8PS, ☎ 602 9851, 9 to 5.30.

Lodging for young people: *Y.H.A.*, Trevelyan House, 8 St. Stephen's Hill, St. Albans, Hertshire, AL1 2DY, ☎ 072755215; *Y.M.C.A.* Accommodation Service, 16 Russell Street, WC1, ☎ 636 4363; *Student Accommodation Services*, 44 Langham Street, W1, ☎ 637 3250.

● *Hotels - Restaurants Shopping*

BATTERSEA

map p. 96-B1

Restaurants:
◆ *Di's Larder*, 62 Lavender Hill, ☎ (01) 223 4618 P ౬ ✍ Cl. 2 wks. Aug., Bank Hols., eves., Sun. Vegetarian cuisine. £4.50.
◆ *Jason's Taverna*, 50 Battersea Park Road, ☎ (01) 622 6998 P ♪ ✍ Cl. 1st, 2nd wks. Aug., Bank Hols., lunch, Sun. Greek cuisine. Book. £8.50.
◆ *La Preferita*, 163 Lavender Hill, ☎ (01) 223 1046, AC AM BA DI ♪ ✍ Cl. 26-30 Dec., Sun. Italian cuisine. Book. £12.
◆ *Ormes*, 245 Lavender Hill, ☎ (01) 228 9824, AC AM BA DI Lunch not served. Cl. Sun. Fish dishes.
◆ *Pollyanna's*, 2 Battersea Rise, ☎ (01) 228 0316, AC AM BA Lunch not served Mon.-Sat. No dinner Sun. Cl. 24-27 Dec. and 1 Jan. £16.

BAYSWATER

map 3-A3

Hotels:
★★★★ *Royal Lancaster* (Rank), Lancaster Terrace, W2 2TY, ☎ (01) 262 6737, Tx 24822, AC AM BA DI, 435 rm. P ⟨ ౬ ✍ £143. Rest. ◆ £17.50.
★★★ *Central Park*, Queensborough Terrace, W2 3SS, ☎ (01) 229 2424, Tx 27342, AC BA AM DI, 287 rm. P £66. Rest. ◆ £9.
★★★ *London Embassy* (Embassy), 150 Bayswater Road, W2 4RT, ☎ (01) 229 1212, Tx 27727, AC AM BA DI, 192 rm. P ౬ £85. Rest. ◆ £12.
★★★ *Park Court* (M.C.H.), 75 Lancaster Gate, W2 3NR, ☎ (01) 402 4272, Tx 23922, AC AM BA DI, 412 rm. ₪ ✍ £69. Rest. ◆ £10.
★★★ *Pembridge Court*, 34 Pembridge Gardens, W2 4DX, ☎ (01) 229 9977, Tx 298363, AC BA AM DI, 35 rm. P £65. Rest. ◆ Cl. Sun., Bank Hols. £11.
★★★ *White's* (M.C.), Lancaster Gate, W2 3NR, ☎ (01) 262 2711, Tx 24771, AC AM BA DI, 61 rm. P £126. Rest. ◆ £26.
★★ *Coburg* (B.W.), 129 Bayswater Road, W2 4RJ, ☎ (01) 229 3654, Tx 268235, AC AM BA DI, 125 rm. £69. Rest. ◆ Cl. Christmas wk. £12.
★★ *Hospitality Inn* (M.C.H.), 104 Bayswater Road, W2 3HL, ☎ (01) 262 4461, Tx 22667, AC AM BA DI, 175 rm. P ⟨ £85. Rest. ◆ £11.
★★ *Mornington* (B.W.), 12 Lancaster Gate, W2 3LG, ☎ (01) 262 7361, Tx 24281, AC AM BA DI, 65 rm. £73.
★ *Allandale*, 3 Devonshire Terrace, W2 3DN, ☎ (01) 723 8311, AC BA DI, 20 rm. ✍ £37.

Restaurants:
● ♦ *Kalamara's*, 76-78 Inverness Mews, ☎ (01) 727 9122, AC AM BA DI ▨ ♪ ❄ Cl. lunch, Christmas eve., Bank Hols., Sun. Seafood in Greek pastry. Book. £14.50.
♦ *Al Khayam*, 27-29 Westbourne Grove, ☎ (01) 727 2556 ♪ ❄ Cl. Christmas. Indian cuisine. Book. £16.
♦ *Bali*, 101 Edgware Road, ☎ (01) 723 3303, AC AM BA DI.
♦ *Bombay Palace*, 2 Hyde Park Square, ☎ (01) 723 8855, AC AM BA DI £13.
♦ *Concordia*, 29-31 Craven Road, ☎ (01) 402 4985, AC AM BA DI Cl. Sun., Bank Hols. £23.
♦ *Fortuna Cookie*, 1 Queensway, ☎ (01) 727 7260.
♦ *Ganges*, 101 Praed Street, ☎ (01) 262 3835, AC AM BA DI Cl. 25-26 Dec. £12.
♦ *Green Jade*, 29-31 Porchester Road, ☎ (01) 229 7221, AC AM BA DI Cl. Sun. lunch.
♦ *Le Mange Tout*, 34 Sussex Place, ☎ (01) 723 1199, AC AM BA DI Cl. Sat. lunch, Christmas, Bank Hols. £19.
♦ *Maharajah*, 50 Queensway, ☎ (01) 727 1135 £13.
♦ *San Marino*, 26 Sussex Place, ☎ (01) 723 8395, AC AM BA DI Cl. Sun., Bank Hols. £18.

Inn or Pub:
Victoria (Charringtons), 10A Strathearn Place, ☎ (01) 262 5696.

Recommended
Cafe: *Pierre Pechon*, 127 Queensway, ☎ (01) 229 0746, choice of over 100 cakes and pastries.
Shopping: *Themes and Variations*, 231 Wesbourne Grove, ☎ (01) 727 5531, Art Deco, fifties furniture and gallery.

BELGRAVIA

map 9-C4

Hotels:
● ★★★★ *Berkeley* (Savoy), Wilton Place, SW1X 7RL, ☎ (01) 235 6000, Tx 919252, AC AM BA DI, 160 rm. ℙ ఉ ❄ ▣ £195. Rest. ♦ Cl. Sat., Sun, Bank Hols. and Aug. £30.
★★★★ *Hyatt Carlton Tower* (Hyatt), 2 Cadogan Place, SW1X 9PY, ☎ (01) 235 5411, Tx 21944, AC AM BA DI, 228 rm. ℙ ❄ £224. Rest. ● ♦ *Chelsea Room*, Cl. 3 days Christmas. £37.
★★★★ *Hyde Park* (T.H.F.), 66 Knightsbridge, SW1Y 7LA, ☎ (01) 235 2000, Tx 262057, AC AM BA DI, 179 rm. ≼ £176. Rest. ♦ *Park Room* ♪ Roast rib of beef. £21.
★★★★ *Lowndes Thistle* (Thistle), 19 Lowndes Street, SW1X 9ES, ☎ (01) 235 6020, Tx 919065, AC AM BA DI, 79 rm. £149. Rest. ♦ £18.
★★★★ *Sheraton Park Tower*, 101 Knightsbridge, SW1X 7RN, ☎ (01) 235 8050, Tx 917222, AC AM BA DI, 295 rm. ℙ ❄ £172. Rest. ♦ ♪ £20.
● ★★★ *Capital*, 22-24 Basil Street, SW3 1AT, ☎ (01) 589 5171, Tx 919042, AC AM BA DI, 60 rm. ℙ £151. Rest. ● ♦ Mousseline of scallops with sea-urchin cream, rack of lamb. £21.
★★★ *Belgravia Sheraton*, 20 Chesham Place, SW1X 8HQ, ☎ (01) 235 6040, Tx 919020, AC AM BA DI, 89 rm. ❄ £158. Rest. ♦ Cl. Sat. lunch. £20.
★★ *Basil Street*, SW3 1AH, ☎ (01) 581 3311, Tx 28379, AC AM BA DI, 94 rm. £99. Rest. ♦ *Dining Room* ♪ Roast beef carved from the trolley. £18.

Restaurants:
● ♦ *Ports*, 11 Beauchamp Place, ☎ (01) 581 3837, AC AM BA DI ♪ ❄ Sun. and Bank Hols. Portuguese dishes, seafood. Book. £17.
● ♦ *Salloos*, 62-64 Kinnerton Street, ☎ (01) 235 4444, AC AM BA DI Cl. Sun. and Bank Hols. Indian cheese soufflé. £25.
● ♦ *San Lorenzo*, 22 Beauchamp Place, ☎ (01) 584 1074 ≼ ఊ Cl. Christmas, Easter, Sun. Italian cuisine. Book. £17.
♦ *Dumpling House*, 9 Beauchamp Place, ☎ (01) 589 8240, AC AM BA DI ❄ Cl. 25-26 Dec. Peking duck, king prawns. £8.50.

♦ *La Fantaisie Brasserie*, 14 Knightsbridge Green, ☎ (01) 589 0509, AC AM BA DI 🍸 ♪ ♫ Cl. Bank Hols., Sun. Book. £16.

♦ *Maroush II*, 38 Beauchamp Place, ☎ (01) 581 5434, AC AM BA DI 🍸 ♪ ♫ Cl. Christmas. Middle Eastern cuisine. Book. £17.50.

♦ *Ménage à Trois*, 15 Beauchamp Place, ☎ (01) 589 4252, AC AM BA DI ♪ Cl. Christmas, Sun. Mousse with caviar, smoked salmon and scallops. Book. £30.

♦ *Mes Amis*, 31 Basil Street, ☎ (01) 584 4484, AC AM BA DI £18.

♦ *Motcombs*, 26 Motcomb Street, ☎ (01) 235 6382, AC AM BA DI Cl. Sun. £16.

♦ *San Martino*, 103 Walton Street, ☎ (01) 589 3833, AC AM BA DI Ⓟ 🍸 ♿ ♫ Cl. Christmas, Easter, Bank Hols., Sun. Pasta dishes. Book. £10.

♦ *San Ruffillo*, 8 Harriet Street, ☎ (01) 235 3969, AC AM BA DI Cl. Sun. and Bank Hols. £15.

♦ *Tent*, 15 Eccleston Street, ☎ (01) 730 6922, AC AM BA Cl. Sat. £12.

Inns or Pubs:
Antelope (Benskins), 22 Eaton Terrace, ☎ (01) 730 7781.
Grenadier (Watneys), 18 Wilton Row, ☎ (01) 235 3074, AC AM BA DI ♫ Traditional English food in restaurant. £18.
Nag's Head (Benskins and Burton), 53 Kinnerton Street, ☎ (01) 235 1135 £4.

Recommended
Cafe: Bendicks, 195 Sloane Street, ☎ (01) 235 4749, coffee, tea and gateaux.
Shopping: Bertjerman and Barton, 43 Elizabeth Street, new boutique of famed teas and teapots;*Fogal*, 51 Brompton Road, sophisticated stockings;*Harvey Nichol's*, Knightsbridge, Lady Di's favourite store;*Jasper Conran*, Beauchamp Place, lingerie;*Max Pike's*, 4 Eccleston Street, bathroom accessories;*Mostly Smoked*, 47 Elizabeth Street, specialized in smoked fish;*Scotch House*, 2 Brompton Road, Scotch classics.
Teashop: Fouquet of Paris, 58 Beauchamp Place, Knightsbridge, ☎ (01) 581 5540, homemade chocolate, teas, coffees, champagnes and jams.
Wine bar: *Carriages*, 43 Buckingham Palace Road, ☎ (01) 434 8871, upmarket wine list.

BLOOMSBURY

map 5-E2

Hotels:
★★★★ *Kenilworth* (E.D.W.), 97 Great Russell Street, WC1B 3LB, ☎ (01) 637 3477, Tx 25842, AC AM BA DI, 180 rm. ♦ £17.

★★★★ *Regent Crest* (Crest), Carburton Street, W1P 8EE, ☎ (01) 388 2300, Tx 22453, AC AM BA DI, 322 rm. Ⓟ ♫ £95. Rest. ♦ £16.

★★★ *Bedford Corner* (Aquarius), Bayley Street, WC1B 3HD, ☎ (01) 580 7766, Tx 296464, AC AM BA DI, 88 rm. £77. Rest. ♦ ♪ Cl. 24 Dec.-1 Jan. £15.

★★★ *Berners*, 10 Berners Street, W1A 3BE, ☎ (01) 636 1629, Tx 25759, AC AM BA DI, 234 rm. ♿ ♫ £115. Rest. ♦ £14.

★★★ *Bloomsbury Crest*, Coram Street, WC1N 1HT, ☎ (01) 837 1200, Tx 22113, AC AM BA DI, 250 rm. Ⓟ £85. Rest. ♦ £12.

★★★ *Grafton* (E.D.W.), 130 Tottenham Court Road, W1P 9HP, ☎ (01) 388 4131, Tx 297234, AC AM BA DI, 178 rm. ♫ £94. Rest. ♦ £11.

★★★ *Kennedy* (M.C.H.), 43 Cardington Street, NW1 2LP, ☎ (01) 387 4400, Tx 28250, AC AM BA DI, 320 rm. Ⓟ ♫ £65. Rest. ♦ £11.

★★★ *Kingsley* (M.C.H.), Bloomsbury Way, WC1A 2SD, ☎ (01) 242 5881, Tx 21157, AC AM BA DI, 146 rm. £80. Rest. ♦ Cl. Sat. and Sun. £14.

★★★ *Royal Scot* (M.C.H.), 100 Kings Cross Road, WC1X 9DT, ☎ (01) 278 2434, Tx 27657, AC AM BA DI, 349 rm. P £65. Rest. ♦ ♪ £10.

★★★ *Russell* (T.H.F.), Russell Square, WC1B 5BE, ☎ (01) 837 6470, Tx 24615, AC AM BA DI, 318 rm. £89. Rest. ♦ £16.

★★★ *St. George's* (T.H.F.), Langham Place, W1N 8QS, ☎ (01) 580 0111, Tx 27274, AC AM BA DI, 85 rm. £120. Rest. ♦ £19.

★★ *Bonnington*, 92 Southampton Row, WC1B 4BH, ☎ (01) 242 2828, Tx 261591, AC AM BA DI, 242 rm. & £68. Rest. ♦ £10.

★★ *Royal National* (Imperial London), Bedford Way, WC1H 0DG, ☎ (01) 637 2488, Tx 21822, AC AM BA DI, 1028 rm. P & £50. Rest. ♦ ♪ & £10.

★ *Crichton*, 36 Bedford Place, WC1B 5JR, ☎ (01) 637 3955, Tx 22353, AC AM BA DI, 64 rm. Listed building. £33.

Restaurants:

● ♦ *Porte de la Cité*, 65 Theobalds Road, ☎ (01) 242 1154, AC AM BA DI ✦ Cl. Christmas, Easter, Bank Hols., eves., Sat. and Sun. Supreme de poulet. Book. £16.50.

● ♦ *Rue St. Jacques*, 5 Charlotte Street, ☎ (01) 637 0222, AC AM BA DI ♪ & ✦ Cl. Sat. lunch., Sun., Easter, Bank Hols, 24 Dec.-5 Jan. Book. £32.

● ♦ *White Tower*, 1 Percy Street, ☎ (01) 636 8141, AC AM BA DI ✦ Cl. 3 wks. Aug., 1 wk. Christmas, Bank Hols., Sat., Sun. Greek dishes, roast duckling. Book. £20.

♦ *Aunties*, 126 Cleveland Street, ☎ (01) 387 1548, AC AM BA DI No lunch Sat. Cl. Sun., 25-26 Dec., 1 Jan. and Bank Hols. £16.

♦ *Cranks*, Tottenham Street, ☎ (01) 631 3912 ♪ ✦ Cl. Bank Hols., Sun. Health food breakfast, quiche, flans, pizza, salads. £7.

♦ *Elephants and Butterflies*, 67 Charlotte Street, ☎ (01) 580 1732, AC AM BA DI ♪ ✦ Cl. Bank Hols., Sat. lunch., Sun. Vegetarian cuisine. Organic ingredients. Book. £9.50.

♦ *Gonbei*, 151 Kings Cross Road, ☎ (01) 278 0619 ♪ ✦ Cl. Sun., 25 Dec.- 1 Jan. Japanese dishes. Sushi. Book. £13.

♦ *Hare Krishna Curry House*, 1 Hanway Street, ☎ (01) 636 5262, AC AM BA DI ✦ ♪ & ✦ Cl. Sun. Hindu vegetarian dishes. £6.

♦ *Lai Qila*, 117 Tottenham Court Road, ☎ (01) 387 4570, AC AM BA DI Cl. 25-26 Dec. £14.

♦ *Les Halles*, 57 Theobalds Road, ☎ (01) 242 6761, AC AM BA DI No lunch Sat. Cl. Sun. and Bank Hols. £25.

♦ *Little Akropolis*, 10 Charlotte Street, ☎ (01) 636 8198, AC AM BA DI No lunch Sat. Cl. Sun. and Bank Hols. Greek cuisine. £10.

♦ *L'Etoile*, 30 Charlotte Street, ☎ (01) 636 7189, AC AM BA DI ✦ Cl. Aug., Bank Hols. French cuisine. Book. £30.

♦ *Mandeer*, 21 Hanway Place, ☎ (01) 323 0660, AC AM BA DI ✦ ♪ ✦ Cl. Bank Hols., Christmas, Sun. Indian vegetarian dishes. Book. £10.

♦ *Mr Kai*, 50 Woburn Place, ☎ (01) 580 1188, AC AM BA DI Cl. 25-26 Dec., 1 Jan. and Bank Hols. £21.

♦ *The Greenhouse*, 16 Chenies Street, ☎ (01) 637 8038 ♪ ✦ Cl. 24 Dec.-1 Jan., Sun. Wholefood and vegetarian dishes. £4.50.

♦ *Winstons Eating House*, 24 Coptic Street, ☎ (01) 580 3422, AM AC BA DI No lunch Sat. No dinner Sun. Cl. Christmas, New Year and Bank Hols.

Inns or Pubs:

Museum Tavern, 49 Great Russell Street, ☎ (01) 242 8987, BA DI Cream teas Mon.-Sat.

Lamb (Youngs), 94 Lambs Conduit Street, ☎ (01) 405 0713.

Recommended

Bicycles: *Condor cycles*, 144 Grays Inn Road, the cream of the crop, possible to make your own bicycle.

Bookshop: *Bloomsbury Rare Books*, 29 Museum Street, an agreeable disorder of rare books.

Shoes: *Sacha*, 351 New Oxford Street, ☎ (01) 499 7272, fashionable shoes for women.

♥ prints: *The Print Room*, 37 Museum Street, enchanting prints, principally on natural history; umbrellas: *James Smith and Son*, 53 New Oxford Street, umbrellas since 1830.

CHELSEA

map 9-B5

Hotels:
★★★★ *Chelsea*, 17-25 Sloane Street, SW1X 9NU, ☎ (01) 235 4377, Tx 919111, AC AM BA DI, 202 rm. ✆ ▨ £118. Rest. ♦ £17.
★★ *Willet*, 32 Sloane Gardens, SW1V 8DJ, ☎ (01) 730 0634, 17 rm. ✆ £37.50.
★ *Fenja*, 69 Cadogan Gardens, SW3 2RB, ☎ (01) 589 1183, AC AM BA DI, 18 rm. ✆

Restaurants:
● ♦ *Beccofino*, 100 Draycott Avenue, ☎ (01) 584 3600, AC AM BA ♪ ✆ Cl. Bank Hols., Sun. Book. £20.
● ♦ *Dans*, 119 Sydney Street, ☎ (01) 352 2718, AC AM BA DI Cl. Sat., Sun., Bank Hols. and 1 wk. Christmas. £15.
● ♦ *English Garden*, 10 Lincoln Street, ☎ (01) 584 7272, AC AM BA DI ♪ ✆ Cl. 25-26 Dec. Quail egg patty. Book. £28.50.
● ♦ *English House*, 3 Milner Street, ☎ (01) 584 3002, AM BA DI AC ⚲ ✆ Cl. 25-26 Dec. Lamb in salt crust. Book. £24.
● ♦ *Gavvers*, 61 Lower Sloane Street, ☎ (01) 730 5983, AM DI No lunch. Cl. Sun. and Bank Hols. £18.
● ♦ *Ma Cuisine*, 113 Walton Street, ☎ (01) 584 7585, AM DI Cl. 14 Jul.-14 Aug., Sat., Sun., Christmas, 1 Jan., 1 wk. Easter. £17.
● ♦ *Ponte Nuovo*, 126 Fulham Road, ☎ (01) 370 6656, AC AM BA DI ⅏ ✆ Cl. Bank Hols. Linguine al cartoccio. Book. £16.
● ♦ *San Frediano*, 62 Fulham Road, ☎ (01) 584 8375, AC BA DI ✆ Cl. Sun. Book. £16.
● ♦ *St. Quentin*, 243 Brompton Road, ☎ (01) 589 8005, AC AM BA DI ✆ Cl. 1 wk. Christmas. Feuilletés d'escargots. Book. £20.
● ♦ *Tante Claire*, 68 Royal Hospital Road, ☎ (01) 352 6045, AM DI ✆ Cl. 1 wk. Christmas, 1 wk. Easter, 3 wks. Aug., Sat., Sun. Galette de foie gras. Book. £36.
● ♦ *Waltons*, 121 Walton Street, ☎ (01) 584 0204, AC AM BA DI Cl. Bank Hols. 'Moneybag' of chicken and asparagus. Book. £29.
♦ *Avoirdupois*, 334 Kings Road, ☎ (01) 352 6151, AC AM BA DI.
♦ *Choy's*, 172 Kings Road, ☎ (01) 352 9085, AC AM BA DI £20.
♦ *Daphne's*, 112 Draycott Avenue, ☎ (01) 589 4257, AC AM BA DI ✆ Cl. Sun., Bank Hols. No lunch. £18.50.
♦ *Don Luigi's*, 316 Kings Road, ☎ (01) 730 3023.
♦ *Eleven Park Walk*, 11 Park Walk, ☎ (01) 352 3449, AC AM DI £21.
♦ *Good Earth*, 233 Brompton Road, ☎ (01) 584 3658 Cl. 24-27 Dec.
♦ *Good Earth*, 91 Kings Road, ☎ (01) 352 9231, AC AM BA DI Cl. 24-27 Dec. £17.
♦ *La Brasserie*, 272 Brompton Road, ☎ (01) 584 1668, AM AC BA DI ♪ ✆ Cl. 25-26 Dec. Book. £12.50.
♦ *Le Français*, 259 Fulham Road, ☎ (01) 352 4748, AM BA ✆ Cl. Christmas, Sun. French regional cuisine. Book. £23.
♦ *Le Suquet*, 104 Draycott Avenue, ☎ (01) 581 1785, AM ✆ Cl. 25 Dec.-4 Jan. Seafood. Book. £40.
♦ *Mario*, 260-262A Brompton Road, ☎ (01) 584 1724, AC AM BA DI Cl. Bank Hols. £14.
♦ *Meridiana*, 169 Fulham Road, ☎ (01) 589 8815, AC AM BA DI ⅏ ♪ ✆ Homemade gnocchi. Book. £22.
♦ *Monkeys*, 1 Cale Street, Chelsea Green, ☎ (01) 352 4711 ✆ Cl. 25-26 Dec., 1 wk. Feb., 3 wks. Aug. Game meats. Book. £15.
♦ *Poissonnerie de l'Avenue*, 82 Sloane Avenue, ☎ (01) 589 2457, AC AM BA DI ⚲ ✆ Cl. Bank Hols., Sun., 24 Dec. - 2 Jan. Seafood. Book. £18.
♦ *Tandoori*, 153 Fulham Road, ☎ (01) 589 7749, AC AM BA DI ℗ ⚲ ♪ ✆ Cl. 25-26 Dec. King prawn, bhuna, masala. Book. £16.
♦ *Thierry's*, 342 Kings Road, ☎ (01) 352 3365, AM BA DI ♪ Cl. last 2 wks. Aug., Bank Hols., Sun., Christmas, Easter. French cuisine. Rack of lamb. Book. £15.

♦ *Toto*, Walton House, Walton Street, ☎ (01) 589 0075, AC AM BA Cl. Easter and 4 days Christmas. £21.
♦ *Zen Chinese*, Chelsea Cloisters, Sloane Avenue, ☎ (01) 589 1781, AC AM BA DI Cl. 25-27 Dec. Old Buddhist dishes. £13.

Inns or Pubs:
Cross Keys (Courage), Lawrence Street. Bar food.
Henry J Bean's, 195-197 Kings Road, ☎ (01) 352 9255 ⌂ ₺ £8.

Recommended
Antique market: *Antiquarius*, 135 Kings Road, covered market with good coffee shop.
Gallery: *Chenil Galleries*, 181 Kings Road, for lovers of Art Deco and Art Nouveau, good cafeteria.
Fashion: *Reiss*, 114 Kings Road, American sportswear; *Stephen King*, 315 Kings Road.
Shoes: *Zapata Shoes Co.*, 49-51 Old Church Street.

CITY

map 6-G3
ⓘ City of London information, St. Paul's Churchyard, ☎ 606 3030.

Hotels:
★★★★ *Tower Thistle* (Thistle), St. Katharine's Way, Tower Hamlets, E1 9LD, ☎ (01) 481 2575, Tx 885934, AC AM BA DI, 826 rm. ℙ £112. Rest. ♦ £20.
★★★ *Great Eastern* (Compass), Liverpool Street, EC2M 7QN, ☎ (01) 283 4363, Tx 886812, AC AM BA DI, 163 rm. £75. Rest. ♦ *City Eates* ♪ Cl. 24 Dec.-2 Jan. Carvery. £9.

Restaurants:
● ♦ *Hana Guruma*, 49 Bow Lane, ☎ (01) 236 6451, AC AM BA DI ♪ ₺ ⅋ Cl. Christmas, 1 Jan., Sat., Sun. Yakitori bar. Book. £13.
● ♦ *Le Poulbot*, 45 Cheapside, ☎ (01) 236 4379, AC AM BA DI ⅋ Cl. Christmas, 1 Jan., Bank Hols., dinner, Sat., Sun. French cuisine. No children under 4. Book. £25.50.
♦ *Baron of Beef*, Gresham Street, ☎ (01) 606 6961, AC AM BA DI ⧫ ♪ ⅋ Cl. Sat., Sun. Sirloin of beef, summer pudding. Book. £30.
♦ *Cafe St. Pierre*, 29 Clerkenwell Green, ☎ (01) 251 6606, AC AM BA DI Cl. Sat., Sun., 24 Dec.- 2 Jan., Bank Hols £17.
♦ *Corney Barrow*, 118 Moorgate, ☎ (01) 628 2898, AC AM BA DI ♪ ⅋ Cl. Christmas, 1 Jan., Easter, Bank Hols., Sat., Sun. Anglo-French cuisine. Book. £13.
♦ *Ginnan*, 5 Cathedral Place, ☎ (01) 236 4120 AC AM BA DI ♪ ⅋ Cl. Bank Hols., Sat. eve., Sun. Japanese cuisine. £18.
♦ *La Bastille*, 116 Newgate Street, ☎ (01) 600 1134, AC AM BA DI Cl. dinner, 1 wk. Aug., 2 wks. Dec. £18.
♦ *Le Gamin*, 32 Old Bailey, ☎ (01) 236 7931, AC AM BA DI Cl. dinner, Sat., Sun., Bank Hols. Book. £19.
♦ *Oscar's Brasserie*, Temple Chambers, Temple Avenue, ☎ (01) 353 6272, AC AM BA DI ⧫ ⧓ ♪ ⅋ Cl. last 3 wks. Aug., last wk. Dec., Bank Hols., Sat., Sun. Turbot marinière, fillet of lamb. Book. £15.
♦ *Shares*, 12-13 Lime Street, ☎ (01) 623 1843 Cl. dinner, Bank Hols. £24.
♦ *The Nosherie*, 12-13 Greville Street, ☎ (01) 242 1591 ⅋ Cl. Sat., Sun. Jewish cuisine. Salt beef, cheese blintzes. £7.
♦ *Wheeler's*, 33 Foster Lane, ☎ (01) 606 0896, AC AM BA DI ♪ ⅋ Cl. Sat., Sun., Mon.-Fri. eve. Fish and seafood. £22.50.

Inns or Pubs:
Black Friar, 174 Queen Victoria Street, ☎ (01) 236 5650. Opulent Art Nouveau and Edwardian decor. Home-cooked lunch ex. Sat.-Sun.
Chiswell Vaults (Whitbreads), Chiswell Street, ☎ (01) 588 5733.
Cock Tavern, The Poultry Market, Central Markets, ☎ (01) 248 2918, AC AM BA DI Breakfast, lunch, snacks eve. £7.50.
Dirty Dick's, 202 Bishopgate, ☎ (01) 283 5888, BA DI.

Fox Anchor (Inde Coope), 115 Chartershouse Street, ☎ (01) 253 4838 P & Breakfast, lunches. £6.50.

Hand Shears (Courage), 1 Middle Street, ☎ (01) 600 0257.

Old Bell Tavern, 95 Fleet Street, ☎ (01) 583 0070.

Old Dr. Butler's Head, Masons Avenue, ☎ (01) 606 3504, BA DI.

Old Wine Shades, 6 Martin Lane.

Olde Chesire Cheese, 145 Fleet Street, ☎ (01) 353 6170 Traditional English menu. £9.

Olde Mitre (Allied), Ely Court, Hatton Garden, ☎ (01) 405 4751 3 rm.

Olde Watling (Vintage), 29 Watling Street, ☎ (01) 248 6235, BA DI.

Printer's Devil (Whitbreads), 98 Fetter Lane, ☎ (01) 242 2239.

Samuel Pepys (Toby-Bass), Brooks Wharf, Upper Thames Street, ☎ (01) 248 3048, AC AM BA DI ⊰ £10.50.

Three Compasses (Trumans), 66 Cowcross Street, ☎ (01) 253 3368.

Windmill (Charringtons), 27 Tabernacle Street, ☎ (01) 638 2603. & £6.

Recommended
Silver: *London Silver Vaults*, incredible number of booths selling antiques, modern silver.
♥ shoes: *Church's English Shoes*, 90 Poultry Street.

EMBANKMENT

map 6-F3

Hotels:
● ★★★★ *Savoy*, The Strand, WC2R 0EU, ☎ (01) 836 4343, Tx 24234, AC AM BA DI, 200 rm. P ⊰ ⊗ £220. Rest. ● ♦ *River*, £26.

★★★★ *Howard* (Barclays), 12 Temple Place, WC2 2PR, ☎ (01) 836 3555, Tx 268047, AC AM BA DI, 141 rm. P ⊰ ⊗ £190. Rest. ♦ *Quai d'Or* ♪ Fillets of sole 'Isle de France'. £30.

★★★★ *Waldorf* (T.H.F.), Aldwych, WC2B 4DD, ☎ (01) 836 2400, Tx 24574, AC AM BA DI, 312 rm. £110. Rest. ♦ Cl. Sat. lunch, Sun. and Bank Hols. Hotel Cl. 24 Dec., 1 Jan. £21.

★★★ *Charing Cross*, P.O. Box 99, The Strand, WC2N 5HX, ☎ (01) 839 7282, Tx 261101, AC AM BA DI, 219 rm. P £85. Rest. ♦ ♪ Cl. 1 wk. Christmas £12.

★★★ *Royal Horseguards* (Thistle), Whitehall Court, SW1A 2EJ, ☎ (01) 839 3400, Tx 917096, AC AM BA DI, 284 rm. ⊰ ⊗ £135. Rest. ♦ £22.

★★★ *Strand Palace* (T.H.F.), The Strand, WC2R 0JJ, ☎ (01) 836 8080, Tx 24208, AC AM BA DI, 775 rm. £81. Rest. ♦ £16.

Restaurants:
● ♦ *Simpsons*, 100 The Strand, ☎ (01) 836 9112, AC AM BA DI ⊗ Cl. Christmas, Easter, Sun., Bank Hols. 3 rm. Roast sirloin of beef. Book. £18.

♦ *Azami*, 13-15 West Street, ☎ (01) 240 0634.

♦ *Cafe Pelican*, 45 St. Martin's Lane, ☎ (01) 379 0309, AC AM BA DI ♨ ♪ ⊗ Cl. 25-26 Dec. Book. £18.

♦ *Cranks*, Unit 11, The Market, Covent Garden, ☎ (01) 379 6508 ⊗ Cl. Bank Hols., Sun. Book. £8.

♦ *Flounders*, 19 Tavistock Street, ☎ (01) 836 3925 Seafood.

♦ *Food for Thought*, 31 Neal Street, Covent Garden, ☎ (01) 836 0239 ⊗ Cl. last wk. Dec.-1st wk. Jan., Bank Hols., Sun. £5.50.

♦ *Laguna*, 50 St. Martin's Lane, ☎ (01) 836 0960, AC AM BA DI Cl. Sun. and Bank Hols. £13.50.

♦ *Le Cafe du Jardin*, 28 Wellington Street, ☎ (01) 836 8769, AC AM BA DI Cl. Sat. lunch, Sun. and Christmas.

♦ *P S Hispaniola*, River Thames, ☎ (01) 839 3011, AC BA DI Cl. 25 Dec.- 1 Jan. No lunch Sat. Restaurant is on board a boat. £18.

♦ *Sheekey's*, 29-31 St. Martin's Court, ☎ (01) 240 2565, AC AM BA DI ⊗ Cl. Christmas, Easter, Bank Hols., Sat. lunch, Sun. Dish of the day. £12.

♦ *Shuttleworth's of Aldwych*, 1 Aldwych, ☎ (01) 836 3346, AC AM BA DI ♪ ⍦ Cl. Bank Hols., Sat. lunch, Sun. Game meats. Scotch steaks. Book. £14.50.
♦ *Taste of India*, 25 Catherine Street, ☎ (01) 836 6591, AC AM BA DI ⍦ ⍦ Book. £17.
♦ *Thomas de Quincey's*, 36 Tavistock Street, ☎ (01) 240 3972, AC AM BA DI No lunch Sat., Cl. Sun., Bank Hols., 3 wks. Aug. £30.

Inns or Pubs:
Lamb & Flag (Courage), 33 Rose Street, Covent Garden, ☎ (01) 836 4108 Bar food with cheese specialities. £2.50.
Punch & Judy (Courage), The Market.
Seven Stars (Courage), 53 Carey Street, ☎ (01) 242 8521.
Sherlock Holmes (Whitbreads), 10 Northumberland Street, ☎ (01) 930 2644.

FINSBURY

map 6-F2

Hotel:
★★★*London Ryan* (M.C.), Gwynne Place, Kings Cross Road, WCIX 9QN, ☎ (01) 278 2480, Tx 27728, AC AM BA DI, 213 rm. Ⓟ ⍦£60. Rest. ♦ £10.

Inn or Pub:
Pheasant Firkin (Bruce's), 166 Goswell Road, ☎ (01) 253 7429.

FULHAM

map p. 96-A1

Restaurants:
● ♦ *Le Gastronome*, 309 New Kings Road, ☎ (01) 731 6993, AC AM BA DI ♪ ⍦ Cl. 25 Dec.-1 Jan., Bank Hols., Sat. lunch, Sun. Desserts. Book. £18.
● ♦ *L'Hippocampe*, 131 Munster Road, ☎ (01) 736 5588, AC AM BA Ⓟ Cl. Sat. lunch, Sun., 24 Dec.-31 Jan. £21.
● ♦ *Perfumed Conservatory*, 182 Wandswth Br. Road, ☎ (01) 731 0732, AC AM BA Cl. Sun., Mon., 1 wk. Christmas and Bank Hols. £20.
♦ *Barbarella*, 428 Fulham Road, ☎ (01) 385 9434, AC AM BA DI ♪ ⍦ Cl. Bank Hols., Sun. Book. £17.
♦ *Hiders*, 755 Fulham Road, ☎ (01) 736 2331, AC AM BA ⍦ Cl. 2 wks. Aug., Sat. lunch, Sun., 25 Dec.-1 Jan., Bank Hols. French cuisine. Crab terrine. Noisette of lamb. Book. £14.50.
♦ *The Garden*, 616 Fulham Road, ☎ (01) 736 6056, AC AM BA DI ♪ Cl. 2-3 wks. Aug., Bank Hols., Sun. Chicken and artichoke pies. Vegetarian dishes. Book. £12.
♦ *Trencherman*, 271 New Kings Road, ☎ (01) 736 4988, AM BA DI French provincial.
♦ *Windmill Restaurant*, 486 Fulham Road, ☎ (01) 385 1570 ♪ ⍦ ⍦ Vegetarian cuisine.

Inns or Pubs:
Ferret Firkin (Bruce's), 114 Lots Road, ☎ (01) 352 6645.
King's Head, Eight Bells (Whitbread), 50 Cheyne Walk, ☎ (01) 352 1820, AC AM BA DI ⍦ Gourmet pies and salads, hot meals and pub food. £5.50.
White Horse (Vintage), 1 Parsons Green, ☎ (01) 736 2115. Breakfast Sat.-Sun. and famous bar meals. £5.

Recommended
♥ *Joseph*, 268 Brompton Road, new line of clothes; *Whittays*, 111 Fulham Road, dozens of varieties of coffee and tea.

HOLBORN

map 6-F3

Hotel:
★★★ *Drury Lane Moat* (Q.M.H.), Drury Lane, WC2B 5RE, ☎ (01) 836 6666, Tx 8811395, AC AM BA DI, 128 rm. Ⓟ ⍦ £99. Rest. ♦ £17.

Inn or Pub:
Princess Louise (Vaux), 208 High Holborn, ☎ (01) 405 8816.

KENSINGTON

map 8-A4

Hotels:
★★★★ *Blakes*, 33 Roland Gardens, SW7 3PF, ☎ (01) 370 6701, Tx 8813500, AC AM BA DI, 50 rm. ✆ £165. Rest. ♦ ♪ Cl. 25-26 Dec. Roast rack of English lamb with rosemary. £33.50.
★★★★ *Gloucester* (Rank), 4 Harrington Gardens, SW7 4LH, ☎ (01) 373 6030, Tx 917505, AC AM BA DI, 531 rm. Ⓟ ᵫ ✆ £126. Rest. ♦ £26.
★★★★ *Hilton Kensington*, 179 Holland Park Avenue, Notting Hill, W11 4UL, ☎ (01) 603 3355, Tx 919763, AC AM BA DI, 606 rm. Ⓟ ᵫ ✆ £120. Rest. ♦ *Market*, £21.
★★★★ *London Tara* (B.W.), Scarsdale Place, Wrights Lane, W8 5SR, ☎ (01) 937 7211, Tx 918834, AC AM BA DI, 830 rm. Ⓟ ᵫ ✆ £80. Rest. ♦ *Poachers* ♪ ᵫ £20.
★★★★ *Portobello*, 22 Stanley Gardens, Notting Hill, W11 2NG, ☎ (01) 727 2777, Tx 21879, AC AM BA DI, 25 rm. £103. Rest. ♦ Cl. 26 Dec.-2 Jan. Residents only. £15.
★★★★ *Royal Garden* (Rank), Kensington High Street, W8 4PT, ☎ (01) 937 8000, Tx 263151, AC AM BA DI, 395 rm. Ⓟ ✆ £150. Rest. ♦ *Royal Roof*, Cl. Sat. lunch, Sun., Bank Hols., lunch, 3 wks. Aug. £23.
★★★ *Alexander* (B.M.H.), 9 Sumner Place, SW7 3EE, ☎ (01) 581 1591, Tx 917133, AC AM BA DI, 38 rm. Ⓟ ₥ ✆ £84. Rest. ♦ £11.50.
★★★ *Baileys*, 140 Gloucester Road, SW7 4QH, ☎ (01) 373 6000, Tx 264221, AC AM BA DI, 70 rm. £78. Rest. ♦ *Bombay Brasserie* ♪ Cl. 26-28 Dec. Indian cuisine. £20.
★★★ *Barkston*, Barkston Gardens, Earl's Court, SW5 0EW, ☎ (01) 373 7851, Tx 8953154, AC AM BA DI, 77 rm. £52.50. Rest. ♦ ♪ £10.
★★★ *Eden Plaza*, 68 Queen's Gate, SW7 5JT, ☎ (01) 370 6111, Tx 916228, AC AM BA DI, 65 rm. £60. Rest. ♦ ♪ £9.50.
★★★ *Forum* (Forum), 97 Cromwell Road, SW7 4DN, ☎ (01) 370 5757, Tx 919663, AC AM BA DI, 907 rm. Ⓟ £84. Rest. ♦ £12.
★★★ *Gore* (B.W.), 189 Queen's Gate, SW7 5EX, ☎ (01) 584 6601, Tx 296244, AC AM BA DI, 57 rm. ✆ £110. Rest. ♦ Cl. Sat. £16.
★★★ *John Howard*, 4 Queen's Gate, SW7 5EH, ☎ (01) 581 3011, Tx 8813397, AC AM BA DI, 40 rm. ✆ £108. Rest. ♦ ♪ Mousse de langouste aux perles de la Caspienne. £23.
★★★ *Kensington Close* (T.H.F.), Wrights Lane, W8 5SP, ☎ (01) 937 8170, Tx 23914, AC AM BA DI, 537 rm. Ⓟ ₥ ▭ Amenities include gym., coffee shop £75. Rest. ♦ £17.
★★★ *Kensington Thistle*, De Vere Gardens, W8 5AF, ☎ (01) 937 8121, Tx 262422, AC AM BA DI, 298 rm. ✆ £107. Rest. ♦ ♪ Cl. Sun. £18.
★★★ *London International* (S.W.A.), 147C Cromwell Road, Earl's Court, SW5 0TH, ☎ (01) 370 4200, Tx 27260, AC AM BA DI, 415 rm. Ⓟ Constructed in air space over District Line on a steel concrete bridge. £68. Rest. ♦ £25.
★★★ *Regency* (Sarova), 100-105 Queen's Gate, SW7 5AG, ☎ (01) 370 4595, Tx 267594, AC AM BA DI, 188 rm. ✆ £87. Rest. ♦ £12.
★★★ *Rembrandt* (Sarova), Thurloe Place, SW7 2RS, ☎ (01) 589 8100, Tx 295828, AC AM BA DI, 200 rm. ✆ ▭ £90. Rest. ♦ £15.
★★★ *Vanderbilt* (E.D.W.), 76 Cromwell Road, SW7 5BT, ☎ (01) 589 2424, Tx 919867, AC AM BA DI, 230 rm. £84. Rest. ♦ ♪ £9.50.
★★ *Hogarth* (I.N.H.), Hogarth Road, Earl's Court, SW5 0QQ, ☎ (01) 370 6831, Tx 8591994, AC AM BA DI, 88 rm. Ⓟ ✆ £50. Rest. ♦ £9.50.

★★ **Lexham**, 32-38 Lexham Gardens, W8 5JU, ☎ (01) 373 6471, Tx 268141, AC BA, 60 rm. ▥ ⌦ £39. Rest. ◆ ♪ Cl. Christmas wk. £7.50.

★★ **Number Sixteen**, 15-17 Sumner Place, SW7 3EG, ☎ (01) 589 5232, Tx 266638, AC AM BA DI, 32 rm. ▥ ⌦ £85.

★★ **Town House**, 44-48 West Cromwell Road, Earl's Court, SW5 9QL, ☎ (01) 373 4546, Tx 918554, AC AM BA DI, 47 rm. ⌦ £55.

★ **Embassy House** (Embassy), 31 Queen's Gate, SW7 5JA, ☎ (01) 584 7222, Tx 8813387, AC AM BA DI, 70 rm. £66. Rest. ◆ Cl. lunch Sat. and Sun. £10.

Restaurants:

● ◆ **Bahn Thai**, 35 Marloes Road, ☎ (01) 937 9960, AC AM DI ⌕ ♪ Cl. 2 wks. Aug., 2 wks. Christmas. Thai cuisine. Book. £12.

● ◆ **Chanterelle**, 119 Old Brompton Road, ☎ (01) 373 5522, AC AM BA DI ⌦ Cl. 4 days Christmas. Book. £13.

● ◆ **Clarke's**, 124 Kensington Church Street, ☎ (01) 221 9225, AC BA Cl. Sat., Sun., 3 wks. Aug., 10 days Christmas, 1 wk. Easter. Char grills. Book. £19.

● ◆ **Hilaire**, 68 Old Brompton Road, ☎ (01) 584 8993, AC AM BA DI ⌦ Cl. Bank Hols., Sat. lunch, Sun. Book. £23.

● ◆ **Kensington Tandoori**, 1 Abingdon Road, ☎ (01) 937 6182, AC AM BA DI.

● ◆ **La Ruelle**, 14 Wrights Lane, ☎ (01) 937 8525, AC AM BA DI Cl. Sat., Sun., Bank Hols. No children under 12. £29.

● ◆ **Read's**, 152 Old Brompton Road, ☎ (01) 373 2445, AC AM BA DI ▥ ⌦ Cl. Christmas, Bank Hols., Sun. dinner. Anglo-french cuisine. Book. £30.

● ◆ **Tiger Lee**, 251 Old Brompton Road, Earl's Court, ☎ (01) 370 2323, AM BA DI AC ♿ ⌦ Cl. Christmas, lunch. Lobster, crispy duck. Book. £22.

◆ **Bombay Brasserie**, Courtfield Close, 140 Gloucester Road, ☎ (01) 370 4040, AC AM BA DI £20.

◆ **Cap's**, 64 Pembridge Road, ☎ (01) 229 5177, AC AM BA DI ♪ ⌦ Cl. Bank Hols., Sun., lunch. 29 rm. Book. £11.

◆ **Chez Moi**, 1 Addison Avenue, ☎ (01) 603 8267, AC AM BA DI ⌕ ⌦ Cl. 2 wks. Aug., Christmas, lunch, Sun. Rack of lamb. Book. £21.

◆ **Crystal Palace**, 10 Hogarth Place, Hogarth Road, Earl's Court, ☎ (01) 373 0754, AC AM BA DI ⌕ ♪ ⌦ Cl. Bank Hols. Peking, Szechuan. £12.50.

◆ **Daquise**, 20 Thurloe Street, ☎ (01) 589 6117 ⌦ Cl. 25-26 Dec. 2 rm. Polish and Russian main dishes. £7.

◆ **Franco Ovest**, 3 Russell Gardens, ☎ (01) 602 1242, AC AM BA DI Cl. Sat. lunch, Sun. Italian. £18.

◆ **Golden Chopsticks**, 1 Harrington Road, ☎ (01) 584 0855 ⌕ ♪ ⌦ Cl. Christmas. Book. £13.

◆ **Hiroko of Kensington**, 179 Holland Park Avenue, ☎ (01) 603 5003, AC AM BA DI Cl. Mon. lunch, 25-26 Dec., 1-4 Jan., Bank Hols. Japanese cuisine. £20.

◆ **Holland Street**, 33C Holland Street, ☎ (01) 937 3224, AC BA ⌦ Cl. Aug., Bank Hols., Sat. lunch, Sun. eve. Chicken breast stuffed with spinach and Stilton cheese. Book. £14.

◆ **I Ching**, 40 Earl's Court Road, ☎ (01) 937 7047.

◆ **Il Barbino**, 32 Kensington Church Street, ☎ (01) 937 8752, AC AM BA DI Cl. Sat. lunch, Sun. £11.

◆ **Julie's**, 135 Portland Road, Holland Park, ☎ (01) 727 4585, AC AM BA DI ▥ ⌕ ♪ ⌦ Cl. 4 days Christmas, Easter, Aug., Bank Hols. Cotswold duck with peaches, port and cherries. Book. £20.

◆ **La Paesana**, 30 Uxbridge Street, ☎ (01) 229 4332, AC BA DI ⌕ ♪ ⌦ Cl. Bank Hols., Sun., 17-20 Apr., 25-26 Dec. Italian cuisine Book. £13.

◆ **La Pomme d'Amour**, 128 Holland Park Avenue, ☎ (01) 229 8532, AC AM BA DI ▥ ⌕ ♿ ⌦ Cl. Bank Hols., Sat. lunch, Sun. Caneton au poivre vert et ananas. Book. £23.

◆ **La Residence**, 148 Holland Park Avenue, ☎ (01) 221 6090, AC AM BA DI Cl. Sat. lunch, Mon. and Bank Hols. £13.

◆ **Le Crocodile**, 38C/D Kensington Church Street, ☎ (01) 938 2501, AC AM BA DI ♪ ⌦ Cl. Sat. lunch, Sun. Boudin de fruits de mer au riz sauvage. Book. £22.

◆ **Le Quai St. Pierre**, 7 Stratford Road, ☎ (01) 937 6388, AM DI Cl. Mon. lunch and Sun.

♦ **Leith's**, 92 Kensington Park Road, ☎ (01) 229 4481, AC AM BA DI ✎ Cl. Christmas 4 days, Bank Hols. Brill fillet stuffed with crab mousseline, lobster sauce. Book. £27.

♦ **Lilly's**, 6 Clarendon Road, ☎ (01) 727 9359, AC AM BA DI ◔ ⦂ ✎ Cl. 1 wk. Christmas. Supreme of halibut with mango banana. Book. £15.

♦ **L'Aquitaine**, 158 Old Brompton Road, Earl's Court, ☎ (01) 373 9918, AC AM BA DI ⦂ ✎ Cl. Sun. Confit de canard à la crème de flageolets. Book. £19.

♦ **L'Artiste Affamé**, 243 Old Brompton Road, Earl's Court, ☎ (01) 373 1659, AC AM BA DI Cl. Sun., 24-26 Dec., Bank Hols.

♦ **L'Artiste Assoiffé**, 122 Kensington Park Road, ☎ (01) 727 4714, AC AM BA DI ℙ ⦂ Cl. Sun. Crab mango. Book. £12.

♦ **Maggie Jones**, Church Street, 6 Old Court Place, ☎ (01) 937 6462, AC AM BA DI Cl. lunch Sun.

♦ **Malabar**, 27 Uxbridge Street, ☎ (01) 727 8800, AC BA ✎ Cl. last 2 wks. Aug., 25-27 Dec. Indian cuisine. Devilled Kaleja (chicken livers). Book. £15.

♦ **Mama San**, 11 Russell Gardens, ☎ (01) 602 0312.

♦ **Mandarin**, 197C High Street, ☎ (01) 937 1551, AC AM BA DI ✎ Cl. 24-25 Dec. Peking duck. Crispy beef. Book. £22.

♦ **Memories of India**, 18 Gloucester Road, ☎ (01) 589 6450, AC AM BA DI ℙ ▦ ⦂ ✎ Cl. 25-26 Dec. King prawn Mahala. Book. £11.50.

♦ **Michel**, 343 Kensington High Street, ☎ (01) 603 3613, AC AM BA DI ✎ French cuisine. Book. £19.

♦ **Monsieur Thompsons**, 29 Kensington Park Road, ☎ (01) 727 9957.

♦ **Montpeliano**, 13 Montpelier Street, ☎ (01) 589 0032 Cl. Sun., Christmas, Bank Hols.

♦ **New Lotus Garden**, 257 Old Brompton Road, Earl's Court, ☎ (01) 370 4450, AM AC BA DI Pekinese.

♦ **New Singapore Mandarin**, 120-122 Holland Park Avenue, ☎ (01) 727 6341, AM BA DI ◔ ⦂ ✎ Cl. Christmas. Book. £12.

♦ **Phoenicia**, 11-13 Abingdon Road, ☎ (01) 937 0120, AC AM BA DI ◔ ⦂ ✎ Cl. 25-26 Dec. Lebanese dishes. Tabouleh. Book. £12.50.

♦ **Pontevecchio**, 254-258 Old Brompton Road, Earl's Court, ☎ (01) 373 9082, AC AM BA DI ✎ Cl. Bank Hols. Italian cuisine. Book. £16.

♦ **Pun Chinese Cuisine**, 53 Old Brompton Road, ☎ (01) 225 1609, AC AM BA DI ✎ Cl. 25-26 Dec. Book. £17.

♦ **Restaurant 192**, 192 Kensington Park Road, ☎ (01) 229 0482, AC AM BA Cl. lunch Sun. £17.

♦ **Sailing Junk**, 59 Melrose Road, ☎ (01) 937 2589, AC AM BA DI Cl. lunch, 25-26 Dec., Good Fri. £14.50.

♦ **Siam**, 12 St. Alban's Grove, ☎ (01) 937 8765, AC AM BA DI ◔ ⦂ ✎ Cl. lunch Mon. and Sat. Siam baked platter. Book. £15.75.

♦ **The Ark**, 36 Kensington Street, ☎ (01) 937 4294, AC AM BA DI ✎ Cl. Sun. lunch., 4 days Christmas, 4 days Easter. Rack of lamb, steak and kidney pie. Book. £10.

♦ **Topo d'oro**, 38 Uxbridge Street, ☎ (01) 727 5813, AC AM BA DI ℙ ⦂ ✎ Cl. 25-26 Dec. Book. £15.

♦ **Trattoo**, 2 Abingdon Road, ☎ (01) 937 4448, AC AM BA DI Cl. Easter and Christmas. Italian. £14.

Inns or Pubs:
Anglesea Arms, 15 Selwood Terrace.
Frog Firkin (Bruce's), 41 Tavistock Crescent, Westbourne Park, ☎ (01) 727 4250 ▦
Narrow Boat (Fullers), 346 Ladbroke Grove ⦂ ▦
Scarsdale Arms (Watneys), 23 Edwardes Square, ☎ (01) 937 4513 ▦
Windsor Castle (Charringtons), 114 Campden Hill Road, ☎ (01) 727 8491, BA ▦ £4.

Recommended
Antique market: Portobello Road, most famous in the world, open Sat. 7-5.
Bookshop: *Waterstone and Co. Ltd.*, 135 Kensington High Street.
Tearoom: *Julie's*, 137 Portland Road, ☎ (01) 727 7987, open until 7 p.m.; *Muffin Man*, Wrights Lane, ☎ (01) 937 6652, open until 7 p.m.

♥ *Hyper Hyper*, Kensington High Street, three floors of booths of jewelry, clothes made by students.

LAMBETH

map 11-F5

Hotel:
★★ *London Park* (Consort), Brook Drive, SE11 4QU, ☎ (01) 735 9191, Tx 919161, AC AM BA DI, 388 rm. P £47. Rest. ♦ £8.

Restaurants:
● ♦ *Chez Nico*, 129 Queenstown Road, ☎ (01) 720 6960, AC BA DI Cl. Sun., Mon., 3 wks. in summer, 1 wk. Christmas, Sat. lunch. Book. £30.
● ♦ *L'Arlequin*, 123 Queenstown Road, ☎ (01) 622 0555, AC AM BA DI Cl. Sat., Sun., Bank Hols., 1 wk. Christmas, 3 wks. Aug. Challand duck with foie gras. Ris de veau et homard. Book. £40.
♦ *Alonso's*, 32 Queenstown Road, ☎ (01) 720 5986, AC AM BA DI Cl. Sat. lunch and Sun. £18.
♦ *Lampwicks*, 24 Queenstown Road, ☎ (01) 622 7800, AM AC BA DI Cl. Sun., Mon., 2 wks. Christmas, last 2 wks. Aug.

MAIDA VALE

Hotel:
★★★ *Colonnade*, 2 Warrington Crescent, W9 1ER, ☎ (01) 289 2167, Tx 298930, AC AM BA DI, 51 rm. P £82. Rest. ♦ Cl. Fri. and Sat. £13.

Restaurant:
♦ *Didier*, 5 Warwick Place, ☎ (01) 286 7484, AC AM BA ⬧ 🜄 ☙ Cl. Bank Hols., Sat., Sun. Book. £15.

MARYLEBONE

map 4-C3

Hotels:
★★★★ *Churchill*, 30 Portman Square, W1A 4ZX, ☎ (01) 486 5800, Tx 264831, AC AM BA DI, 489 rm. P 🔥 ☙ ⌁ £162. Rest. ♦ £32.
★★★★ *Cumberland* (T.H.F.), Marble Arch, W1A 4RF, ☎ (01) 262 1234, Tx 22215, AC AM BA DI, 905 rm. 🔥 ☙ £110. Rest. ♦ *Wyvern* ♪ 🔥 Cl. 26 Dec., 1 Jan. £19.
★★★★ *Marble Arch* (Holiday Inn), 134 George Street, W1H 6DN, ☎ (01) 723 1277, Tx 27983, AC AM BA DI, 241 rm. P 🔥 🖾 £130. Rest. ♦ *La Bibliothèque* 🔥 Cl. lunch, Sun., Bank Hols. Steak 'Lucien', scampi maître d'hôtel. £20.
★★★★ *Mount Royal* (M.C.H.), Bryanston Street, W1A 4UR, ☎ (01) 629 8040, Tx 23355, AC AM BA DI, 700 rm. Amenities: coffee shop, shopping arcade. £76. Rest. ♦ £12.
★★★★ *Portman Inter-Cont* (I.N.C.), 22 Portman Square, W1H 9FL, ☎ (01) 486 5844, Tx 261526, AC AM BA DI, 276 rm. P 🔥 ⌁ Modern brick hotel. Amenities: coffee shop, air conditioning, theatre desk, secretarial agency. £150. Rest. ♦ £25.
★★★★ *Selfridge* (Thistle), 400 Orchard Street, W1H 0JS, ☎ (01) 408 2080, Tx 22361, AC AM BA DI, 298 rm. P 🔥 Modern hotel behind the Oxford Street store of the same name. Air conditioning. Restaurants and coffee shop. £165. Rest. ♦ £25.
★★★★ *White House* (Rank), Regent's Park, NW1 3UP, ☎ (01) 387 1200, Tx 24111, AC AM BA DI, 580 rm. £100. Rest. ♦ ♪ Cl. Sat. lunch, Sun., Bank Hols. £22.
★★★ *Bryanston Court*, 56-60 Great Cumberland Place, W1H 7FD, ☎ (01) 262 3141, Tx 262076, AC AM BA DI, 56 rm. ☙ £63. Rest. ♦ £14.
★★★ *Clifton Ford*, 47 Welbeck Street, W1M 8DN, ☎ (01) 486 6600, Tx 22569, AC AM BA DI, 220 rm. P £99. Rest. ♦ Roast rib of beef from the trolley. £18.

★★★ *Concorde*, 50 Great Cumberland Place, W1H 7FD, ☎ (01) 402 6169, Tx 262076, AC AM BA DI, 28 rm. ✝ £50. Rest. ♦ ♪ Cl. Sat., Sun. £13.

★★★ *Durrants*, 26-32 George Street, W1H 6BJ, ☎ (01) 935 8131, Tx 894919, AC AM BA DI, 102 rm. ✝ Georgian building built 1789. £81. Rest. ♦ £17.

★★★ *Harewood*, Harewood Row, Regent's Park, NW1 6SE, ☎ (01) 262 2707, Tx 297225, AC AM BA DI, 93 rm. ✝ £70. Rest. ♦ *Street Cars* ♪ Grill only. £9.

★★★ *Londoner* (Sarova), 57-59 Welbeck Street, W1M 8HS, ☎ (01) 935 4442, Tx 894630, AC AM BA DI, 142 rm. ✝ £90. Rest. ♦ ♪ Cl. Sat., Sun. lunch. £11.

★★★ *Mandeville*, Mandeville Place, W1M 6BE, ☎ (01) 935 5599, Tx 269487, AC AM BA DI, 164 rm. £94.50. Rest. ♦ £16.

★★★ *Montcalm*, Great Cumberland Place, W1A 2LF, ☎ (01) 402 4288, Tx 28710, AC AM BA DI, 116 rm. £150. Rest. ♦ *La Varenne* ♪ Veal kidneys with wild mushrooms. £25.

★★★ *Mostyn* (Sarova), Portman Street, W1H 0DE, ☎ (01) 935 2361, Tx 27656, AC AM BA DI, 123 rm. Parts date back 200 years. Adam ceilings in restaurant. £90. Rest. ♦ £10.

★★★ *Stratford Court* (E.D.W.), 350 Oxford Street, W1N 0BY, ☎ (01) 629 7474, Tx 22270, AC AM BA DI, 138 rm. ✝ £94. Rest. ♦ ♪ Coffee-shop and carvery. £10.

★ *Hallam*, 12 Hallam Street, W1N 5LJ, ☎ (01) 580 1166, AC AM BA DI, 23 rm. ✝ £53.

★ *Portman Court*, 30 Seymour Street, 5WD W1H, ☎ (01) 402 5401, AC AM BA DI, 30 rm. ✝ £47.

Restaurants:

● ♦ *Langan's Bistro*, 26 Devonshire Street, ☎ (01) 935 4531, AM ◷ ✝ Cl. Christmas, Bank Hols., Sat. lunch, Sun. French cuisine. Chocolate pudding. Book £25.

● ♦ *Le Muscadet*, 25 Paddington Street, ☎ (01) 935 2883, AC BA ♪ ✝ Cl. Sun., 1-21 Aug., 2 wks. Christmas, Bank Hols., Sat. lunch. Book. £13.

● ♦ *Odin's*, 27 Devonshire Street, ☎ (01) 935 7296, AM ✝ Cl. Christmas, 1 Jan., Sat. lunch, Sun. Anglo-French. Book. £25.

♦ *Asuka*, Berkeley Arcade, 209A Baker Street, ☎ (01) 486 5026, AC AM BA DI Cl. Sat. lunch, Sun., 24 Dec.- 5 Jan. Japanese cuisine. £40.

♦ *Biagi's*, 39 Upper Berkeley Street, ☎ (01) 723 0394, AC AM BA DI ✝ Cl. Bank Hols. Italian cuisine. Book. £12.

♦ *Caravan Serai*, 50 Paddington Street, ☎ (01) 935 1208, AC AM BA DI ℗ ◷ ♪ ♦ ✝ Cl. Sun. lunch. Middle-Eastern cuisine. Ashak. Book. £8.

♦ *Chaopraya*, 22 St. Christopher's Place, ☎ (01) 486 0777, AC AM BA DI Cl. Sat. lunch, Sun. and Bank Hols. Thai cuisine. £15.

♦ *Defune*, 61 Blandford Street, ☎ (01) 935 8311, AM DI ◷ ♪ ✝ Cl. 10 days Dec., Bank Hols., Sun. Japanese cuisine. Sushi, sashimi. Book. £23.

♦ *Del Monico's*, 114 Crawford Street, ☎ (01) 935 5736, AC AM BA DI ♪ ✝ Cl. 25-26 Dec., 1 Jan., Sun. Italian cuisine. Book. £16.50.

♦ *Gaylord*, 79 Mortimer Street, ☎ (01) 580 3615, AC AM BA DI ℗ ◷ ♪ ✝ Indian and Pakistani cuisine. Book. £12.

♦ *Geneviève*, 13 Thayer Street, ☎ (01) 935 5023, AC AM BA DI ◷ ✝ Cl. Bank Hols., Sat., Sun. French cuisine. Guinea fowl in pastry with ginger sauce. Book. £11.50.

♦ *Kerzenstuberl*, 9 St. Christopher's Place, ☎ (01) 486 3196, AC AM BA DI Cl. Sat. lunch, Sun., Christmas, Bank Hols., 3 Aug.- 3 Sep. Austrian cuisine. £20.

♦ *La Pavona*, 5-7 Blandford Street, ☎ (01) 486 9696 Italian cuisine.

♦ *Masako*, 6-8 St. Christopher's Place, ☎ (01) 935 1579, AM AC BA DI Cl. Sun., Christmas, 3 days New Year, Easter, Bank Hols. Japanese cuisine.

♦ *Raw Deal*, York Street, ☎ (01) 262 4841 ◷ ♪ ✝ Cl. Bank Hols., Sun. Vegetarian cuisine. £5.

♦ *Sidi Bou Said*, 9 Seymour Place, ☎ (01) 402 9930, AC AM BA ♪ ✝ Cl. Sun. Couscous. Book. £8.

♦ *Topkapi*, 25 Marylebone High Street, ☎ (01) 486 1872, AC AM BA DI ◷ ♪ ♦ ✝ Cl. 25-26 Dec. Middle-Eastern cuisine. Lamb kebab. Book. £9.

♦ *Viceroy of India*, 3 Glentworth Street, ☎ (01) 486 3401, AC AM BA DI ♪ ⅋ Cl. Christmas. Indian cuisine-Bataire masala (quail). Book. £11.

Inn or Pub:
George, 55 Great Portland Street, ☎ (01) 636 0863.
Nag's Head (Mc Muller), 10 James Street, ☎ (01) 836 4678.

Recommended
Bed and breakfast: *Merryfield House*, 42 York Street, ☎ (01) 935 8326. £32 double; B. & B.
Gallery: *Diorama*, 18 Park Square East, ☎ (01) 487 2896, where unknown artists can get their first break.
Tearoom: *Maison Sagne*, 105 Marylebone High Street, ☎ (01) 935 6240, since 1921, Italian style decor.
Wine bar: *Crawfords*, 10-11 Crawford Street, ☎ (01) 486 0506, cold buffets available from £3.95, popular and agreeable.
♥ *Ixi*, 14-15 Stratford Place, St. Christopher's Place, casual sportswear;*Miss Selfridge*, 400 Oxford Street, satisfy your wildest dreams cheaply;*Nicole Fahri*, 26 St. Christopher's Place, elegant, conservative clothes for business women;*Squash*, 29 St. Christopher's Place, reasonably priced fashion for the young; *W. H. Models*, 11 Cavendish Mews, Ali Baba's cave for model-lovers.

MAYFAIR

map 4-C1
ℹ️ LTB travel information at Selfridges Department Store, Oxford Street.
Car-rental: Avis, 68 North Row, ☎ 629 7811.

Hotels:
● ★★★★ *Athenaeum* (Rank), 116 Piccadilly, W1V 0BJ, ☎ (01) 499 3464, Tx 261589, AC AM BA DI, 112 rm. ⅋ £165. Rest. ♦ £24.
● ★★★★ *Brown's* (T.H.F.), Albemarle Street, W1A 4SW, ☎ (01) 493 6020, Tx 28686, AC AM BA DI, 125 rm. £155. Rest. ♦ *L'Aperitif*, £24.
● ★★★★ *Claridge's*, Brook Street, W1A 2JQ, ☎ (01) 629 8860, Tx 21872, AC AM BA DI, 205 rm. ♿ ⅋ £195. Rest. ♦ Cl. Sat., Bank Hols. £30.
● ★★★★ *Connaught* (Savoy), 16 Carlos Place, W1Y 6AL, ☎ (01) 499 7070, AC, 90 rm. ⅋ £140. Rest. ● ♦ £35.
● ★★★★ *Dorchester*, 53 Park Lane, W1A 2HJ, ☎ (01) 629 8888, Tx 887704, AC AM BA DI, 280 rm. Ⓟ ♿ ⅋ £185. Rest. ● ♦ *Terrace Room*, Cl. Sun. £38.
● ★★★★ *Intercontinental* (I.N.C.), 1 Hamilton Place, Hyde Park Corner, W1V 0QY, ☎ (01) 409 3131, Tx 25853, AC AM BA DI, 490 rm. Ⓟ ⅋ £190. Rest. ● ♦ *Le Soufflé* ♪ Cl. Sat. lunch. Savoury and sweet soufflés, veal mignon and sweetbreads. £20.
★★★★ *Britannia* (I.N.C.), Grosvenor Square, W1A 3AN, ☎ (01) 629 9400, Tx 23941, AC AM BA DI, 356 rm. Ⓟ ⅋ Amenities include coffee shop, shopping arcade. £136. Rest. ♦ *Best of Both Worlds*, £20.
★★★★ *Chesterfield*, 35 Charles Street, W1X 8LX, ☎ (01) 491 2622, Tx 269394, AC AM BA DI, 114 rm. ⅋ £115. Rest. ♦ £20.
★★★★ *Grosvenor House* (T.H.F.), Park Lane, W1A 3AA, ☎ (01) 499 6363, Tx 24871, AC AM BA DI, 472 rm. Ⓟ ⅋ ⌧ Once the home of the Grosvenor family. Designed by Edwin Lutgens. Recently modernized. Largest ballroom in Europe. £170. Rest. ♦ Cl. Sat. lunch, Sun. and Bank Hols. £40.
★★★★ *Inn on the Park*, Hamilton Place, Park Lane, W1A 1AZ, ☎ (01) 499 0888, Tx 22771, AC AM BA DI, 228 rm. Ⓟ ♿ £200. Rest. ♦ *Lanes and Four Seasons*, £30.
★★★★ *London Hilton*, 22 Park Lane, W1A 2HH, ☎ (01) 493 8000, Tx 24873, AC AM BA DI, 501 rm. Ⓟ ≼ ♿ £190. Rest. ♦ *British Harvest* ♪ ♿ £34.
★★★★ *May Fair* (I.N.C.), Stratton Street, W1A 2AN, ☎ (01) 629 7777, Tx 262526, AC AM BA DI, 322 rm. ⅋ £177. Rest. ♦ *Le Chateaubriand* ♪ Cl. Sat. lunch. £25.

★★★★ *Mayfair* (Holiday Inn), Berkeley Street, W1X 6NE, ☎ (01) 493 8282, Tx 24561, AC AM BA DI, 185 rm. P ⌘ Restaurant. air conditioning. £133. Rest. ♦ £35.

★★★★ *New Piccadilly* (Gleneagles), Piccadilly, Westminster, W1V 0BH, ☎ (01) 734 8000, Tx 25795, AC AM BA DI, 290 rm. ⌘ 🖃 £165. Rest. ♦ £20.

★★★★ *Park Lane*, Piccadilly, W1Y 8BX, ☎ (01) 499 6321, Tx 21533, AC AM BA DI, 32 rm. P Art Deco ballroom of outstanding interest. Tea time pianist. £140. Rest. ♦ *Bracewells*, £20.

★★★★ *Westbury* (T.H.F.), New Bond Street, W1A 4UH, ☎ (01) 629 7755, Tx 24378, AC AM BA DI, 242 rm. ♿ £132. Rest. ♦ ♪ £26.

★★★ *London Marriott* (Marriott), Grosvenor Square, W1A 4AW, ☎ (01) 493 1232, Tx 268101, AC AM BA DI, 228 rm. P ♿ coffee shop. £160. Rest. ♦ *Diplomat*, £25.

★★★ *Washington* (Sarova), Curzon Street, W1Y 8DT, ☎ (01) 499 7030, Tx 24540, AC AM BA DI, 164 rm. ⌘ £90. Rest. ♦ £20.

★★ *Ladbroke Curzon* (L.A.D.), Stanhope Row, Park Lane, W1Y 7HE, ☎ (01) 493 7222, Tx 24665, AC AM BA DI, 7rm. P £110.

Restaurants:

● ♦ *Al Hamra*, 31-33 Shepherd Market, ☎ (01) 493 1954, AC AM BA DI ⚬ ♪ ♿ ⌘ Cl. 25 Dec.- 1 Jan. Lebanese cuisine. Kibbeh, varnia. Book. £12.

● ♦ *Greenhouse*, 27A Hay's Mews, ☎ (01) 499 3331, AC AM BA DI ⌘ Cl. 25 Dec.-1 Jan., Bank Hols., Sat. lunch, Sun. Roast rack of lamb. Book. £27.

● ♦ *Ho-Ho*, 29 Maddox Street, ☎ (01) 493 1228, AC AM BA DI ♪ ⌘ Cl. Sun. Chinese cuisine. Steamed scallops. No children under 6. Book. £23.

● ♦ *Langan's Brasserie*, Stratton Street, ☎ (01) 491 8822, AC AM BA DI ♪ ⌘ Cl. Christmas, Easter, Bank Hols., Sat. lunch, Sun. Grilled sea bass with herb butter sauce. Book. £17.

● ♦ *Le Gavroche*, 43 Upper Brook Street, ☎ (01) 408 0881, AC AM BA DI ⌘ Cl. Bank Hols., Sat., Sun.,24 Dec.-1 Jan. Caneton Gavroche, l'Assiette du chef, soufflé suisse. No children under 6. Book. £40.

● ♦ *One Two Three*, 27 Davies Street, ☎ (01) 409 0750, AC AM BA DI ♪ ⌘ Cl. Christmas, 1 Jan., Sat., Sun. Japanese cuisine. Book. £30.

♦ *Champagne Exchange*, 17C Curzon Street, ☎ (01) 493 4490, AC AM BA DI ♪ Cl. Sat., Sun. lunch. Caviar, smoked fish, shellfish. Book. £25.

♦ *Gaylord*, 16 Albermarle Street, ☎ (01) 580 3615, AC AM BA DI ⚬ ♪ ⌘ Cl. 25-26 Dec. Indian and Pakistani dishes. £10.

♦ *Golden Carp*, 8A Mount Street, ☎ (01) 499 3385, AC AM BA DI ♪ ⌘ Cl. Bank Hols., Sat. lunch, Sun. £17.

♦ *Guinea Grill*, 26 Bruton Place, ☎ (01) 499 1210, AM AM BA DI ⚬ ⌘ Cl. Sat. lunch, Sun. Steaks. Book. £30.

♦ *Hard Rock Cafe*, 150 Old Park Lane, ☎ (01) 629 0382 ⌘ Hamburgers, chips and salads, smoked pork. £8.

♦ *Ikeda*, 30 Brook Street, ☎ (01) 629 2730, AC AM BA DI Cl. Sat., Sun. Japanese cuisine. £30.

♦ *Justin de Blank*, 54 Duke Street, ☎ (01) 629 3174 ⌘ Cl. Bank Hols., Sat. eve., Sun. Anglo-French cuisine. Lamb and aubergine casserole. £10.

♦ *Library*, 115 Mount Street, ☎ (01) 499 1745, AC AM BA DI Cl. Sat., Sun., Christmas, 1 Jan. £16.

♦ *Marquis*, 121A Mount Street, ☎ (01) 499 1256, AC AM BA DI ⌘ Cl. Bank Hols., Sun. International cuisine. Game in season. Book. £13.

♦ *Mirabelle*, 56 Curzon Street, ☎ (01) 499 4636 ⚍

♦ *Miyama*, 38 Clarges Street, ☎ (01) 499 2443, AC AM BA DI ♪ ⌘ Cl. Easter, Bank Hols., Sat. lunch, Sun, 25 Dec.-1 Jan. Japanese cuisine. Book. £30.

♦ *Mr Kai of Mayfair*, 65 South Audley Street, ☎ (01) 493 8988, AC BA DI ⚬ ♪ ⌘ Cl. 25-26 Dec., Bank Hols. Chinese cuisine. Peking duck. Book. £8.

♦ *Ninety Park Lane*, 90 Park Lane, ☎ (01) 409 1290, AC AM BA DI P ♪ ⌘ Cl. Bank Hols., Sat. lunch, Sun. 325 rms. No children under 6. Book. £42.

♦ *Relais des Amis*, 17B Curzon Street, ☎ (01) 499 7595, AC AM BA DI £19.

♦ **Scotts**, 20 Mount Street, ☎ (01) 629 5248, AC AM BA DI ℗ ⌕ ⌘ Cl. Christmas, Easter, Bank Hols., Sun. lunch. Fish. Supreme de turbotin teymour. Book. £35.

♦ **Shogun**, Adams Row, ☎ (01) 493 1255 Japanese cuisine.

♦ **Tandoori of Mayfair**, 37A Curzon Street, ☎ (01) 629 0600, AC AM BA DI ⦰ ♪ ⌘ Cl. 25-26 Dec. Fish tikka, Sah boti. Book. £14.

♦ **The Magic Moment**, 233 Regent Street, ☎ (01) 734 2251, AC AM BA DI ♪ ⌘ Clam chowder, chargrilled prime rib. Book. £14.

♦ **Tiberio**, 22 Queen Street, ☎ (01) 629 3561, AC AM BA DI Cl. Sat. lunch and Sun. Italian dishes. £25.

♦ **Trader Vic's**, London Hilton, 22 Park Lane, ☎ (01) 493 7586, AC AM BA DI Cl. Sat. lunch, Christmas. Polynesian cuisine. £37.

♦ **Trattoria Fiori**, 87-88 Mount Street, ☎ (01) 499 1447, AC AM BA DI Cl. Sun., Bank Hols. Italian dishes. £26.

Inns or Pubs:
Audley (Clifton), 41 Mount Street, ☎ (01) 499 1843, AC AM BA DI Bar and restaurant food. £10.
Bunch of Grapes, 16 Shepherd Market, ☎ (01) 629 4989 ⅙ Lunches: set price for unlimited quantity. £8.
Guinea, 30 Bruton Street, ☎ (01) 499 1210, AC AM BA DI Grill-room restaurant. £20.
Red Lion (Watneys), 1 Waverton Street, ☎ (01) 499 1307 Bar food and restaurant.

Recommended
Bookshop: *Hatchards*, 187 Piccadilly, ☎ (01) 437 3924.
Confectioners: *Charbonnel et Walker*, 2 Knight's Arcade, Brompton Road, ☎ (01) 581 3117, set up by Edward VII (then Prince of Wales);*Prestat*, 40 South Molton Street, ☎ (01) 629 4838, wide range of handmade truffles, fudge, Turkish delights.
Fashion: *Aquascutum*, 100 Regent Street, classic high quality for men;*Browns*, 23/27 South Molton Street, European style, high prices;*H. Huntsman and Sons*, 3 Burlington Arcade, ☎ (01) 734 7441, classic clothes for men;*Hawes Curtis*, 8 Burlington Gardens, favourite shirtmaker of Prince Charles;*James Drew*, 3 Burlington Arcade, ☎ (01) 493 0714, classic women's clothes;*N. Pealm*, 37 Burlington Arcade, great assortment of cashmeres;*Nutters of Saville Row*, 11 Saville Row, ☎ (01) 437 6850, classic clothes for men;*Swaine Adenyard Brigg*, 185 Piccadilly, chic outdoor clothes;*W . Bill*, 93 New Bond Street, real shetland sweaters.
Jewelers: *Asprey's*, 166 New Bond Street, silver and gold.
Shopping: *Hamley's*, 200 Regent Street, toystore for children and adults.
Tearoom: *Richoux*, 41 South Audley Square, ☎ (01) 629 5228, Victorian atmosphere;*The Palm Court Room*, The Ritz, Piccadilly, ☎ (01) 493 8181, tea dances held in this ornate-ceilinged room with fountain.
♥ shoes: *Church and Co.*, 58-59 Burlington Arcade, ☎ (01) 493 8307;*Maxwell's*, 11 Saville Row, ☎ (01) 734 9714, shoes for men; *Russell and Bromley*, 24 New Bond Street, ☎ (01) 629 6903.

PADDINGTON

map 3-A3
Car-rental: Godfrey Davis Rail Drive, Paddington Station, ☎ 262 5655.

Hotel:
★★★★ **London Metropole**, Edgware Road, W2 1JU, ☎ (01) 402 4141, Tx 23711, AC AM BA DI, 586 rm. ℗ ⌕ ⌘ Coffee shop. £90. Rest. ♦ £19.

Restaurants:
● ♦ **Maroush**, 21 Edgware Road, ☎ (01) 723 0773, AC AM BA DI ♪ ⌘ Cl. Christmas. Middle-Eastern cuisine. Book. £11.
♦ **Canaletto da Leo**, 451 Edgware Road, ☎ (01) 262 7027 Cl. Sat. lunch, Sun. Italian cuisine. £16.

♦ **Knoodles**, 30 Connaught Street, ☎ (01) 262 9623, AC AM BA DI ⌕ ⌘ Cl. Bank Hols., Sun. International cuisine. Homemade pasta dishes. Book. £11.50.
♦ **Trat-West**, 43 Edgware Road, ☎ (01) 723 8203, AC AM BA DI Cl. Sun., Easter, Christmas. Italian cuisine.
♦ **Veronica's Chez Franco**, 3 Hereford Road, ☎ (01) 229 5079, AC AM BA DI Cl. Sat. lunch, Sun., Bank Hols.

PIMLICO

map 10-D5

Hotel:
  Elizabeth, 37 Eccleston Square, SW1V 1PB, ☎ (01) 828 6812, 25 rm. ⌕ ⌘ ⌐ £52.

Restaurants:
● ♦ **Pomegranates**, 94 Grosvenor Road, ☎ (01) 828 6560, AC AM BA DI ⌕ ⌘ Cl. Bank Hols., Sat. lunch, Sun. Jamaican curried goat, gravlax. Book. £25.
♦ **Hunan**, 51 Pimlico Road, ☎ (01) 730 5712 £12.
♦ **La Fontana**, 101 Pimlico Road, ☎ (01) 730 6630, AM BA DI ⌘ Cl. Bank Hols. International cuisine. Book. £16.

Inn or Pub:
Orange Brewery, 37 Pimlico Road, ☎ (01) 730 5378, AM DI.

Recommended
♥ *Mr Fish*, 52 Pimlico Road, clothes from the sixties.

SOHO

map 5-D3

ⓘ London Transport travel information, Oxford Circus, Piccadilly Circus; British Travel Centre, 12 Lower Regent Street.

Restaurants:
● ♦ **Gay Hussar**, 2 Greek Street, ☎ (01) 437 0973 ⌕ ⌘ Cl. Bank Hols., Sun. Hungarian dishes. Book. £21.
● ♦ **New World**, 1 Gerrard Place, ☎ (01) 734 0677, AC AM BA DI ⌘ Cl. Christmas. Lobster with chilli black bean sauce. £7.
● ♦ **Poon's**, 4 Leicester Street, ☎ (01) 437 1528 ℙ ⌘ Cl. Christmas, Sun. Deep-fried squid with chopped garlic, wind-dried food mix, Cantonese dishes. Book. £25.
● ♦ **Red Fort**, 77 Dean Street, ☎ (01) 437 2525, AC AM BA DI ⌕ ⌘ Cl. 25-26 Dec., 1 Jan. Indian cuisine. Tandoori quails. Book. £13.
● ♦ **Soho Brasserie**, 23-25 Old Compton Street, ☎ (01) 439 9301, AC AM BA DI ⌘ Cl. Sun. French cuisine. Magret de canard in sherry vinegar sauce. Book. £13.
♦ **Arirang**, 31 Poland Street, ☎ (01) 437 6633, AC AM BA DI Cl. Sun., Easter-Mon., Christmas.
♦ **Au Jardin Des Gourmets**, 5 Greek Street, ☎ (01) 437 1816, AC AM BA DI ⌕ ⌘ Cl. Sun. lunch, Sun. eve., Christmas, Easter, Bank Hols. 2 rms. French cuisine. Fricassée de poissons au safran. Book. £28.
♦ **Beotys**, 79 St. Martin's Lane, ☎ (01) 836 8768, AC AM BA DI ⌕ ⌘ Cl. Bank Hols., Sun. Greek dishes. Book. £15.50.
♦ **Brewer Street Buttery**, 56 Brewer Street, ☎ (01) 437 7695 ⌘ Cl. Bank Hols., Sat., Sun. 1 rm. Polish cuisine. Pieroshki, bigos. £5.25.
♦ **Cafe Royal (Grill Room)**, 68 Regent Street, ☎ (01) 439 6320, AC AM BA DI Cl. Sun. £30.
♦ **Chesa (Swiss Centre)**, 10 Wardour Street, ☎ (01) 734 1291, AC AM BA DI ℙ ⌘ Cl. 25-26 Dec. Fondue, air-cured meats, bratwurst, chocolate mocca, orange mousse. Book. £24.
♦ **Chiang Mai**, 48 Frith Street, ☎ (01) 437 7444, AC AM BA DI Thai. £10.
♦ **Cork Bottle Wine Bar**, 44-46 Cranbourn Street, ☎ (01) 734 7807, AC BA DI ⌘ Cl. 25-26 Dec., 1 Jan. Raised creamy ham and cheese pie. £7.

♦ *Country Life Vegetarian Buffet*, 123 Regent Street, ☎ (01) 434 2922 ⌕ ✇ Cl. Bank Hols., Sat., Sun. Vegetarian cuisine. £3.50.

♦ *Cranks*, 8 Marshall Street, ☎ (01) 437 9431, AC AM BA DI ♪ ✇ Cl. Bank Hols., Sun. Vegetarian cuisine. £8.

♦ *Desaru*, 60-62 Old Compton Street, ☎ (01) 734 4379, AC AM BA DI ♪ ✇ Cl. 25-26 Dec., 1 Jan. Indonesian and Malaysian cuisine. Book. £12.

♦ *Estoril da Luigi e Roberto*, 3 Denman Street, ☎ (01) 437 8700, AC AM BA DI ♪ ✇ Venison. Book £15.

♦ *Frith's*, 14 Frith Street, ☎ (01) 439 3370, AC AM BA DI ♪ ✇ Cl. Bank Hol. eve., Sat. lunch, Sun. Salmon trout with bread and orange sauce. Book. £18.

♦ *Fuji*, 36 Brewer Street, ☎ (01) 734 0957, AC AM BA DI Cl. lunch Sat., Sun., 2 wks. Christmas. Japanese dishes. £26.

♦ *Fung Shing*, 15 Lisle Street, ☎ (01) 437 1539, AC AM BA DI £14.

♦ *Gallery Rendezvous*, 53-55 Beak Street, ☎ (01) 734 0445, AC AM BA DI ⌕ ♪ ✇ Cl. Christmas, 1 Jan. 3 rms. Chinese cuisine. Barbecued Peking duck. Book. £12.

♦ *Grahame's Seafare*, 38 Poland Street, ☎ (01) 437 3788, BA ♿ ✇ Cl. last wk. Dec., 1st wk. Jan. Jewish style. Halibut with egg lemon sauce. Book. £8.

♦ *Han Kuk Hoe Kwan*, 2 Lowndes Court, Carnaby Street, ☎ (01) 437 3313, AC AM BA DI ♪ ♿ ✇ Cl. 3 days Christmas, 1 Jan., Sun. Bulgoggi — thin sliced beef. Book. £26.

♦ *Il Passetto*, 230 Shaftesbury Avenue, ☎ (01) 836 9391, AC AM BA DI Cl. Sun. £21.

♦ *Joy King Lau*, 3 Leicester Square, ☎ (01) 437 1132 £19.

♦ *Kaya*, 22 Dean Street, ☎ (01) 437 6630, AC AM BA DI Cl. lunch Sat. and Sun. £22.

♦ *La Bastide*, 50 Greek Street, ☎ (01) 734 3300, AC AM BA DI ✇ Cl. Bank Hols., Sat. lunch, Sun. Salmon with sorrel sauce. Book. £17.

♦ *La Corée Korean*, 56 St. Giles High Street, ☎ (01) 836 7235, AC AM BA Cl. Sun., Bank Hols., 3 days Christmas, 2 days New Year.

♦ *La Cucaracha*, 12 Greek Street, ☎ (01) 734 2253, AC AM BA DI Cl. Christmas.

♦ *Lee Ho Fook*, 15 Gerrard Street, ☎ (01) 734 9578, AC AM BA DI ✇ Cl. Christmas, 1 Jan. Duck. £11.

♦ *Leoni's Quo Vadis*, 26-29 Dean Street, ☎ (01) 437 9585, AC AM BA DI Cl. Sat. and Sun. lunch, Christmas, 1 Jan. £19.

♦ *L'Escargot*, 48 Greek Street, ☎ (01) 437 2679, AC AM BA DI ♪ ♿ ✇ Cl. Christmas, 1 Jan., Bank Hols., Sat. lunch, Sun. Book. £20.

♦ *Mayflower*, 66-70 Shaftesbury Avenue, ☎ (01) 734 9027, AC AM BA DI.

♦ *Melati*, 21 Great Windmill Street, ☎ (01) 437 2745, AC AM BA DI ♪ ♿ ✇ Cl. Christmas. Malaysian dishes. Satay, Singapore laksa. Book. £10.

♦ *Nuthouse*, 26 Kingly Street, ☎ (01) 437 9471 ✇ Cl. Sun. Vegetarian cuisine. £4.

♦ *Old Budapest*, 6 Greek Street, ☎ (01) 437 2006, AC AM BA ⌔ ⌕ ♪ ✇ Cl. Christmas, Sun., Bank Hols. Smoked goose, red cabbage, Pungen beans. Book. £15.

♦ *Pizza Express*, 29 Wardour Street, ☎ (01) 437 7215, AC ♪ Pizza veneziana. £4.25.

♦ *Rugantino*, 26 Romilly Street, ☎ (01) 437 5302, AC AM BA DI ♪ ♿ ✇ Cl. Sat. lunch, Sun. Italian cuisine sea bass in pernod and fennel-seed sauce. £14.

♦ *Saigon*, 45 Frith Street, ☎ (01) 437 7109, AM BA DI ♪ ✇ Cl. Bank Hols., Sun. SE Asian dishes. Vietnamese barbecued beef. Book. £15.

♦ *The Diamond*, 23 Lisle Street, ☎ (01) 437 2517.

♦ *Wheeler's*, 19 Old Compton Street, ☎ (01) 437 2706, AC AM BA DI ♪ ✇ Fish and seafood. Book. £22.50.

♦ *Wong Kei*, 41-43 Wardour Street, ☎ (01) 437 3271 ♿ ✇ Cl. Christmas. Soya chicken. £5.

Inn or Pub:
Salisbury, 90 St. Martin's Lane, ☎ (01) 836 5863.

Recommended
Fashion: *Marvelette*, 4 Rupert Court, ☎ (01) 436 9656, the best for secondhand 1940s and 1950s clothes; *Powell and Co.*, 11 Archer Street, ☎ (01) 734 5051, modern vision of 1960s suits.

Nightclub: *Reptile House*, 146 Charing Cross Road, ☎ (01) 240 2261, on Sat. at the Wispers, from 10.30 p.m. to 3 a.m.;*Sacrosanct*, Shaftesbury Avenue, ☎ (01) 734 2017, on Tue. at Shaftesbury's from 10.30 p.m. to 3 a.m.;*The 100 Club*, 100 Oxford Street, ☎ (01) 636 0933, the best jazz club in London, from 7.30 p.m. till after 12 midnight;*The Marquee*, 90 Wardour Street, ☎ (01) 437 6603, most famous rock'n roll place in Europe since 1950;*Whisky a Go-Go*, 35 Wardour Street, ☎ (01) 437 5534, on Tue. at the Wag from 10.30 p.m. to 3 a.m.
Tearoom: *Maison Bertaux*, 44 Old Compton Street, ☎ (01) 437 6007, since 1871, a popular little tearoom overlooking Soho;*Patisserie Valerie*, 44 Old Compton Street, ☎ (01) 437 3466, a tiny Belgian cafe serving coffee, tea, brioches pastries.
Wine bar: *Shampers*, 4 Kingly Street, ☎ (01) 437 1692, best bargains here are Australian and New Zealand wines.

SOUTHWARK

map 6-G4

Restaurants:
● ♦ *Mabileau*, 61 The Cut, ☎ (01) 928 8645, AC AM BA DI ♪ ✕ Cl. Christmas, 1 Jan., Sat. lunch, Sun. French cuisine. Book. £18.
● ♦ *RSJ*, 13A Coin Street, ☎ (01) 928 4554 ♪ ✕ Cl. 2 days Christmas, Bank Hols., Sat. lunch, Sun. Fresh salmon with saffron cream sauce. Book. £16.
♦ *Dining Room*, Winchester Walk, off Cathedral Street, ☎ (01) 407 0337 Cl. Sat., Sun., Mon. Vegetarian. £11.
♦ *South of the Border*, Joan Street, ☎ (01) 928 6374, AC AM BA DI ℗ ⅏ ⚓ ♪ ✕ Cl. Sat. lunch. Australasian, Indonesian, South Pacific cuisine. Book. £16.

Inns or Pubs:
Anchor (Courage), 1 Bankside, ☎ (01) 407 1577, AC AM BA DI ℗ ≼ ⅏ Restaurant and barbecue food. £13.
Founders Arms (Youngs), 52 Hopton Street, Bankside, ☎ (01) 928 1899, AC BA ℗ ≼ ⅏ ♿ £7.
George Inn (Whitbread Fremling), 77 Borough High Street, ☎ (01) 407 2056, AC AM BA DI ✕ The last of London's galleried coaching inns. £11.50.
Goose Firkin (Bruce's), 47 Borough Road, ☎ (01) 403 3590.
Hole in the Wall, 5 Mepham Street.
Market Porter, 9 Stoney Street, ☎ (01) 407 2495, AC BA ✕ Pub food and restaurant. £8.

Recommended
Garden: *Dulwich Park*, a rock garden, sculpture by Hepworth.
Wine bar: *Bar du Musée*, 17 Nelson Road, serves imaginative hot and cold dishes with wine.

ST. GILES

map 5-E3

Restaurants:
● ♦ *Boulestin*, 1A Henrietta Street, ☎ (01) 836 7061, AC AM BA DI ✕ Cl. last 3 wks. Aug., 1 wk. Christmas, Bank Hols. French cuisine. Pigeon and mushrooms. Book. £30.
● ♦ *Inigo Jones*, 14 Garrick Street, ☎ (01) 836 6456, AC AM BA DI ⚓ ✕ Cl. Bank Hols., Sat. lunch, Sun. French cuisine. Book. £40.
● ♦ *Neal Street*, 26 Neal Street, ☎ (01) 836 8368, AC AM BA DI ✕ Cl. 25 Dec.-2 Jan., Sat., Sun., and Bank Hols. Truffles in season, wine-mushroom soup. Book. £28.
● ♦ *Poons of Covent Garden*, 41 King Street, ☎ (01) 240 1743, AC BA DI ✕ Cl. Sun., 24-27 Dec. Lap yuck soom, Kam. Ling duck. Book. £17.50.
● ♦ *Tourment d'Amour*, 19 New Row, ☎ (01) 240 5348, AC AM BA DI ♪ ✕ Cl. 2 wks. Christmas, Bank Hols., Sat. lunch, Sun. No children under 10. Book. £21.

♦ *Chez Solange*, 35 Cranbourne Street, ☎ (01) 836 0542, AC AM BA DI ♪ ⅋ Book. £18.

♦ *Frères Jacques*, 38 Long Acre, ☎ (01) 836 7823, AC AM BA DI Seafood. £19.

♦ *Grimes*, 6 Garrick Street, ☎ (01) 836 7008, AC AM BA DI ♪ ⅋ Cl. Sat. lunch, Sun. Fish. Colchester oysters. Book. £15.

♦ *Interlude de Tabaillau*, 7-8 Bow Street, ☎ (01) 379 6473, AC AM BA DI Cl. 15 Aug.- 7 Sep. Sun., Bank Hols., 2 wks. Christmas, 10 days Easter.

♦ *La Provence*, 8 Mays Court, ☎ (01) 836 9180, AC AM BA DI ♪ ⅋ Cl. Sat. lunch, Sun. Supreme de volaille aux framboises. Book. £16.

♦ *Last Days of The Raj*, 22 Drury Lane, ☎ (01) 836 1628, AC AM BA DI.

♦ *Le Cafe des Amis du Vin*, 11-14 Hanover Place, ☎ (01) 379 3444, AC AM BA DI Cl. Sun. and Christmas.

♦ *L'Opera*, 32 Great Queen Street, ☎ (01) 405 9020, AC AM BA DI ⌕ ♪ ⅋ Cl. Bank Hols., Sat. lunch, Sun. French cuisine. Book. £22.

♦ *Magno's Brasserie*, 65A Long Acre, ☎ (01) 836 6077, AC AM BA DI Cl. Sat. lunch, Sun. and 24 Dec.- 2 Jan. £19.

♦ *Mon Plaisir*, 21 Monmouth Street, ☎ (01) 836 7243, AC AM BA Cl. Sat. lunch, Sun. and Bank Hols. £14.

♦ *Plummers*, 33 King Street, ☎ (01) 240 2534, AC AM BA DI ♪ ⅋ Cl. Sat. lunch, Sun. British dishes. Clam chowder, salmon pie. Book. £13.

♦ *Rules*, 35 Maiden Lane, ☎ (01) 836 5314, AC AM BA DI ⌕ ⅋ Cl. 24 Dec.-1 Jan., Bank Hols., Sun. Book. £16.

Recommended
Fashion: *Colin Swift*, 48 Monmouth Street, superb display of fashion and women's hats;*S. Fischer*, 18 The Market, classic shoes, all colours, cableknit sweaters for men;*The Scottish Merchant*, 16 New Row, handknitted sweaters;*Westaway and Westaway*, 62-65 Great Russell Street, huge selection of woolens in many colours;*Whistles*, 20 The Market, feminine and casual.
Nightclub: *Ascension*, 14 Leicester Square, ☎ (01) 734 4111, Thu., from 10.30 p.m. to 3 a.m. £4.
Shopping: *World*, 27 Litchfield Street, ☎ 379 5588, boutique with clothes, hats, jewels from around the world.
Wine bar: *Bar des Amis*, 11-14 Hanover Place, ☎ (01) 379 3444, a popular basement bar Cl. Sun., £5, wide range of wines.
♥ kite: *The Kite Shop*, 69 Neal Street, wide variety; natural foods: *Neal's Yard Wholefood Warehouse*, 21-23 Short Gardens, jams, honey, wholewheat.

ST. JAMES'S

map 4-D3
ⓘ London Transport travel information, St. James's Park.

Hotels:
● ★★★★ *Dukes* (Prestige), 35 St. James's Place, SW1A 1NY, ☎ (01) 491 4840, Tx 28283, AC AM BA DI, 51 rm. ⌕ £160. Rest. ♦ Chicory parcels filled with brill on light red wine sauce. £30.

★★★★ *Cavendish* (T.H.F.), Jermyn Street, SW1Y 6JF, ☎ (01) 930 2111, Tx 263187, AC AM BA DI, 253 rm. Ⓟ £125. Rest. ♦ £24.

★★★★ *Ritz*, Piccadilly, W1V 9DG, ☎ (01) 493 8181, Tx 267200, AC AM BA DI, 128 rm. ⅋ £200. Rest. ♦ ♪ Skewered Oban scampi in fish mousse on saffron sauce. £35.

★★★ *Pastoria*, St. Martin's Street, WC2H 7HL, ☎ (01) 930 8641, Tx 25538, AC AM BA DI, 52 rm. ⅋ £82.

★★★ *Royal Trafalgar* (Thistle), Whitcomb Street, WC2H 7HG, ☎ (01) 930 4477, Tx 298564, AC AM BA DI, 108 rm. £107. Rest. ♦ ♪ £15.

Restaurants:
● ♦ *Green's*, 36 Duke Street, ☎ (01) 930 4566, AC AM BA DI ♪ ⅋ Cl. Sat., Sun. Fish cakes, English puddings. Book. £16.

● ♦ *Suntory*, 72-73 St. James's Street, ☎ (01) 409 0201, AC AM BA DI ⅋ Cl. Bank Hols. Japanese cuisine. Teppan-yaki, Shabu-shabu. Book. £32.50.

♦ **Le Caprice**, Arlington House, Arlington Road, ☎ (01) 629 2239, AC AM BA DI ♪ ⚄ Cl. 24 Dec.- 2 Jan., Sat. lunch. Noisettes d'agneau bergère. Book. £16.
♦ **Maxim's de Paris**, 32 Panton Street, ☎ (01) 839 4809.

Inns or Pubs:
Red Lion (Watney Combe Reid), 23 Crown Passage, ☎ (01) 930 8067, £6.
Two Chairmen (Courage), 1 Warwick House Street, ☎ (01) 930 1166.

Recommended
Bookshops: *Design Centre*, 28 Haymarket, excellent selection on design;*Foyle's*, 119 Charing Cross Road, the widest choice in London.
Fashion: *James Lock*, 6 St. James's Street, renowned hatmaker.
Nightclub: *BPM*, Hungerford Lane, off Grosvenor Street, from 10:30 p.m.-3 a.m. on Thu. at the Sanctuary.
Shoes: *Lobbs*, 9 St. James's Street, since 1700, famous bootmaker.
Shopping: *Burberry's*, 18 Haymarket, raincoats.

ST. JOHN'S WOOD

map 3-A2

Hotel:
★★★★ **Ladbroke Westmoreland**, 18 Lodge Road, NW8 7JT, ☎ (01) 722 7722, Tx 23101, AC AM BA DI, 347 rm. ℗ £108. Rest. ♦ £14.

Restaurants:
● ♦ **Au Bois St. Jean**, 122 High Street, ☎ (01) 722 0400, AC BA ♪ ⚄ Cl. Christmas, Easter, Sat. lunch. Avocat Cannoise. Book. £15.
♦ **Don Pepe**, 99 Frampton Street, ☎ (01) 262 3834, AC AM BA DI ℗ ♪ ⚄ Cl. 24-25 Dec. Spanish food. Merluza a la Gallega. £15.
♦ **Fortuna Garden**, 128 Allitsen Road, ☎ (01) 586 2391, AC AM BA DI Peking cuisine.
♦ **Lords Rendezvous**, 24 Finchley Road, ☎ (01) 722 4750, AM AC BA DI ⚄ Cl. 25-26 Dec. Chinese. Book. £25.
♦ **L'Aventure**, 3 Blenheim Terrace, ☎ (01) 624 6232, AM Cl. lunch Sat., dinner Sun.
♦ **Oslo Court**, Prince Albert Road, ☎ (01) 722 8795, AC AM BA DI Cl. dinner Sun.

Inns or Pubs:
Crockers (Vaux), 24 Aberdeen Place.
Clifton (Taylor Walker), 96 Clifton Hill, ☎ (01) 624 5233, AC BA ⚅ Country Food menu. £8.

ST. PANCRAS

map 5-E2

ⓘ London Transport travel information, Kings Cross/St. Pancras Underground.
Car-rental: Budget, British Rail Kings Cross, ☎ 833 0972.

Hotels:
★★★ **New Ambassadors**, 12 Upper Woburn Place, WC1H 0JH, ☎ (01) 387 1456, Tx 267074, AC AM BA DI, 101 rm. ⚄ £45. Rest. ♦ ♪ £7.50.
★★ **Great Northern** (Compass), Kings Cross, N1 9AN, ☎ (01) 837 5454, Tx 299041, AC AM BA DI, 87 rm. ℗ £75. Rest. ♦ ♪ Cl. 25 Dec.-1 Jan. Prime roast beef, traditional steak and kidney pie. £9.

STOCKWELL

Restaurant:
♦ *Twenty Trinity Gardens*, 20 Trinity Gardens, ☎ (01) 733 8838, BA Ⓟ ⌕ ♪ ⊗ Cl. Christmas, 1 Jan., Sun. and Sat. lunch. Book. £15.

VICTORIA

map 10-D4

ⓘ London Transport travel information, Victoria Station forecourt; Victoria Underground, ☎ 222 1234.
Car-rental: Budget, Victoria NCP car park, Semley Place ☎ 730 5233; Hertz, Victoria coach station, ☎ 730 8323.

Hotels:
● ★★★★ *Goring*, 15 Beeston Place, Grosvenor Gardens, SW1W 0JW, ☎ (01) 834 8211, Tx 919166, AC AM BA DI, 100 rm. Ⓟ ⊗ First hotel in the world to have central heating and a private bath for each bedroom. £129. Rest. ♦ ♪ £18.
★★★ *Royal Westminster* (Thistle), 49 Buckingham Palace Road, SW1W 0QT, ☎ (01) 834 1821, Tx 916821, AC AM BA DI, 134 rm. £149. Rest. ♦ £23.
★★★ *St. Ermin's* (Stakis), Caxton Street, SW1H 0QW, ☎ (01) 222 7888, Tx 917731, AC AM BA DI, 296 rm. Ⓟ £104. Rest. ♦ Carvery, £13.
★★★ *St. James Court*, Buckingham Gate, SW1E 6AF, ☎ (01) 834 6655, Tx 919557, AC AM BA DI, 400 rm. Ⓟ £155. Rest. ♦ ♪ Fillet of salmon with aubergines. £26.
★★ *Hamilton House*, 60 Warwick Way, SW1V 1SA, ☎ (01) 821 7113, Tx 28604, AC AM BA, 41 rm. £47. Rest. ♦ ♪ £6.50.
★★ *Rubens* (Sarova), 39-41 Buckingham Palace Road, SW1W 0PS, ☎ (01) 834 6600, Tx 916757, AC AM BA DI, 172 rm. £98. Rest. ♦ £12.

Restaurants:
● ♦ *Ciboure*, 21 Eccleston Street, ☎ (01) 730 2505, AC AM BA DI ⊗ Cl. 1 wk. Christmas, Sat. lunch, Sun. French cuisine. Leek mushroom mousse, scallops. No children under 10. Book. £25.
● ♦ *Ken Lo's Memories of China*, 67 Ebury Street, ☎ (01) 730 7734, AC AM BA DI ⊗ Cl. Bank Hols., Sun., Peking duck. Book. £26.
● ♦ *Le Mazarin*, 30 Winchester Street, ☎ (01) 828 3366, AC DI AM ⏣ ♪ Cl. Christmas, Bank Hols., Sun. Book. £22.
● ♦ *Mijanou*, 143 Ebury Street, ☎ (01) 730 4099, AC AM DI ⏣ ⊗ Cl. Sat., Sun., 3 wks. Aug., 2 wks. Christmas, 1 wk. Easter. French cuisine. Cailles au riz sauvage. Book. £17.
● ♦ *Simply Nico,* 48 A Rochester Row, ☎ (01) 630 8061, AC AM BA DI Cl. Sat., Sun., 3 wks. Aug and 1 wk Christmas. French rest. Book. £30.
♦ *Bumbles*, 16 Buckingham Palace Road, ☎ (01) 828 2903, AC AM BA DI Cl. Sat. lunch, Sun., Bank Hols. Scotch rump steak. Book. £14.
♦ *Dolphin Brasserie*, Rodney House, Dolphin Square, Chichester Street, ☎ (01) 828 3207, AM AC BA DI £19.
♦ *Eatons*, 49 Elizabeth Street, ☎ (01) 730 0074, AC AM BA DI ♪ ⊗ Cl. Sat., Sun. and Bank Hols. French cuisine. Smoked salmon, fresh herrings. Book. £17.
♦ *Gran Paradiso*, 52 Wilton Road, ☎ (01) 828 5818, AC AM BA DI Cl. Sat. lunch, Sun., Bank Hols. £13.
♦ *La Poule au Pot*, 231 Ebury Street, ☎ (01) 730 7763, AC AM BA DI Lunch not served Sat. Cl. Sun.
♦ *Methuselah's*, 29 Victoria Street, ☎ (01) 222 0424, AC AM BA DI ♪ ♿ ⊗ Cl. Bank Hols., Sat., Sun. Book.
♦ *Mimmo d'Ischia*, 61 Elizabeth Street, ☎ (01) 730 5406 £14.
♦ *Santini*, 29 Ebury Street, ☎ (01) 730 4094, AC AM BA DI Cl. lunch Sat. and Sun. £19.

♦ *Villa Medici*, 35 Belgrave Road, ☎ (01) 828 3613, AC
AM BA DI Cl. Sat. lunch, Sun. and Bank Hols. £14.

Inns or Pubs:
Buckingham Arms (Youngs), 62 Petty France,
☎ (01) 222 3386 Lunchtime snacks.
Albert (Host), 52 Victoria Street, ☎ (01) 222 5577.

WEST BROMPTON

map p. 96-A2

ⓘ LTB travel information at Harrods Department Store
(4th floor), Brompton Road.

Restaurants:
● ♦ *Bagatelle*, 5 Langton Street, ☎ (01) 351 4185, AC
AM BA DI ❀ Cl. Bank Hols., Sun. and 1 wk. Christmas.
Rack of lamb with mustard sauce. Book. £21.
● ♦ *La Croisette*, 168 Ifield Road, ☎ (01) 373 3694,
AM ❀ Cl. Mon., Tue. lunch, 2 wks. Christmas. Seabass.
Book. £21.
● ♦ *L'Olivier*, 116 Finborough Road, ☎ (01) 370 4183,
AC AM BA DI ⌂ ♪ ❀ Cl. Sun., 2 wks. Christmas.
Book. £25.
♦ *Brinkley's*, 47 Hollywood Road, ☎ (01) 351 1683, AC
AM BA DI Cl. Sun., lunch. £14.

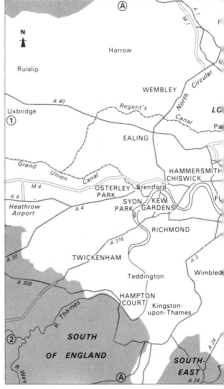

♦ *Chelsea Wharf*, Lots Road, ☎ (01) 351 0861, AC AM BA DI No lunch Mon. Cl. Bank Hols.
♦ *Nikita's*, 65 Ifield Road, ☎ (01) 352 6326, AC AM BA DI Cl. Sun., Christmas and Bank Hols. Russian. £21.
♦ *September*, 457 Fulham Road, ☎ (01) 352 0206, AC AM BA DI Cl. Sun., no lunch. £14.50.
♦ *T'ang*, 294 Fulham Road, ☎ (01) 351 2599 Oriental.

WESTMINSTER

map 10-D4

Restaurants:
♦ *Kundan*, 3 Horseferry Road, ☎ (01) 834 3434, AC AM BA DI ◊ ♪ ⊗ Cl. Bank Hols., Sun. Indian cuisine. Book. £14.50.
♦ *Lockets*, Marsham Street, ☎ (01) 834 9552, AC AM BA DI Cl. Sat. lunch, Sun. and Bank Hols. £16.
♦ *L'Amico*, 44 Horseferry Road, ☎ (01) 222 4680, AC AM BA DI Cl. Sat. and Sun. No children under 4. £16.
♦ *Tate Gallery*, Millbank Embankment, ☎ (01) 834 6754 ⊗ Cl.24-26 Dec., 1 Jan., Sun., 1 May and Good Fri. British dishes. Book. £19.

Inn or Pub:
St. Stephen's Tavern (Whitbreads), 10 Bridge Street, ☎ (01) 930 3230 ⊗ Homemade soups and salads.

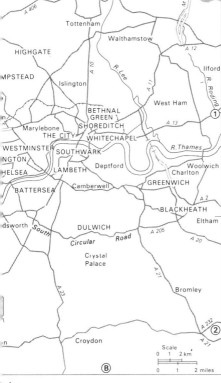

ndon

● *Practical holiday guide*

Getting to Britain

Air travel

Most major airlines serve **London Heathrow** (LHR — the world's busiest international airport) or **Gatwick** (GTW). As well as the regular all-year-round services to these two airports, scheduled flights also operate from many parts of the world direct to Britain's other international airports — **Edinburgh, Glasgow, Luton, Birmingham, Manchester, Bristol, Cardiff** and **Belfast**. Where there is no direct service to the area you wish to visit, you can usually transfer to a domestic service that will take you to your destination or within easy reach of it. Airlines sell seats at a wide variety of prices subject to various pre-conditions. The cheaper the ticket, the more restrictions and qualifications are applied both before and after the flight.

From USA

In the USA, direct flights to Great Britain are available from Atlanta, Boston, Chicago, Dallas/Fort Worth, Los Angeles, New York and San Francisco, among others. Airlines offering regularly scheduled flights from the USA to Great Britain, the majority on a daily basis, are: Air India, Air New Zealand, American Airlines, British Airways, British Caledonian, Continental, Delta, El Al, Kuwait Airways, Northwest Orient, Pan Am, TWA, Virgin Atlantic and World. All scheduled flights land at London Heathrow, Gatwick, Manchester International or Prestwick. There are several fare categories offered by scheduled carriers from the USA to Great Britain: 1st class, business, economy and advance purchase excursion (APEX).

● **Concorde:** a luxurious, supersonic jet flown by British Airways. It only flies from New York, Washington DC and Miami except on special charters. Information can be obtained from most travel agents or British Airways offices.

● **Virgin Atlantic:** a carrier well known for low-cost transatlantic flights (Newark-London Gatwick twice weekly off-season, daily in summer). Information and reservations: ☎ 201 623 0500 or call 800 555 1212 for the airline's toll-free number for your area.

● **Passenger service information:** Information on flights serving specific international airports is available at the following numbers: London (Heathrow): 01-759 4321; (Gatwick): 0293 28822 or 01-668 4211; Glasgow: 041-887 1111; Edinburgh: 031-333 1000; Luton: 0582 31231; Birmingham: 021-767 5511; Manchester: 061-489 3000; Bristol: 0275 87 4441; Cardiff: 0446 711211; Belfast: 0232 229271.

● **Sky Guide:** Up-to-the-minute flight information 'direct' from the seven major airports and a number of the smaller regional airports is available on Prestel through American Express. Key ★2691 for details.

● **Air Taxis:** Information concerning Air Taxi charter throughout the UK can be obtained from the *Air Transport Operators' Association* (☎ 0428 4804).

● **British Airways offices in Britain:** head office: PO Box 10, Heathrow Airport London, Hounslow, Middlesex TW6 2JA (☎ 01-759 5511); BA Gatwick: ☎ 0293 518033.

● **British Airways offices in the USA:** New York: 212 687 1600; Chicago: 312 332 7744; Los Angeles: 213 272 8866; Washington DC: 207 393 5300.

Information

● Aer Lingus: 01-734 1212; Aeroflot: 01-493 7436; Air Canada: 01-759 2636; Air France: 01-499 9511; Air India: 01-491 7979; Air New Zealand: 01-930 3434; Air Portugal: 01-828 0262; Alitalia: 01-602 7111; American Airlines: 01-834 5151; Austrian Airlines: 01-439 0741; British Caledonian: 01-668 4222; Cathay Pacific: 01-930 7878; Delta Airlines: 01-668-0935; Eastern: 0223 517 622; Egyptair: 01-734 2395; El Al: 01-437 9255; Finnair: 01-408 1222; Gulf Air: 01-409 0191; Japan Airlines: 01-408 1000; KLM: 01-750 9000; Lufthansa: 01-408 0442; Malaysian Airlines: 01-491 4542; Middle East Airlines: 01-493 5681; Northwest: 01-629 5353; Olympic: 01-846 9080; Pan Am: 01-409 0688; Qantas: 01-748 5050; Royal Air Maroc: 01-439 8859; Sabena: 01-437 6950; SAS: 01-734 9841; Singapore: 01-439 8111; Swissair: 01-439 4144; TAP: 01-734 4282; TWA: 01-636 4090; Varig Brazilian Airlines: 01-629 5824; Virgin Atlantic: 0293 38222; World: 01-434 3252.

Other airline reservations in London

Although it may be more convenient for some visitors to fly direct to a provincial airport, by far the most popular are London's Heathrow and Gatwick. Both are linked to central London by frequent public transport services. London Heathrow is 15 miles west of central London, linked

Arrival in Britain

by bus and subway (with one underground stop for Heathrow's Terminals 1, 2 and 3, another for Terminal 4). Heathrow lies at the end of the Piccadilly line and the journey to central London takes approximately 45 minutes.

London Transport operates three **Express Airbus** services (☎ 01-222 1234 5am-11pm, 6:45am on Sun.) that run at approximately 10-minute intervals connecting Heathrow to three of London's main railway stations — Victoria (A1), Paddington (A2) and Euston (A3). Journey time is approximately 40 minutes. All the major hotel areas in central London are served and the three routes offer 18 pick-up points.

Car rental is available at Heathrow, as are taxis, the most expensive form of public transport.

Gatwick is a mainline 30-minute train ride from Victoria. Trains run every 15 minutes between 6am and midnight (once an hour throughout the night).

QE2

The most luxurious transatlantic ship is Cunard's Queen Elizabeth II which operates between New York and Southampton (occasionally via Cherbourg in northern France) between April and December. Cunard air/sea packages, combining a one-way crossing with a return flight on Concorde, are also available in conjunction with British Airways. Information: USA: Cunard, 555 Fifth Avenue, New York NY 10017 (☎ (212) 661 7777/(800) 221 4770); London: The Cunard Steam-Ship Company Ltd, 30-35 Pall Mall, London W1Y 5LS (☎ 01 491 3930).

Ferries

Some ten ferry companies (plus one hydrofoil and two hovercraft services) operate a total of 32 services linking Britain to the rest of Europe. The majority carry cars, campers, trailers, caravans, motorcycles and bicycles, as well as passengers. The two major ferry companies, **Sealink/British Ferries** and **P. and O.,** plus **Hoverspeed,** run a virtual shuttle service at ten-minute intervals during the summertime rush hours. Journey times vary from the speedy half-hour hovercraft trip across the English Channel to the 24-hour and longer, more leisurely North Sea crossing in one of the larger cruise-style ships. About a third of the total cross-Channel traffic is via Dover-Calais, the shortest, quickest, most popular ferry route (1 hour 30 minutes). Considerable savings can often be made by traveling off-season or choosing a mid-week sailing during the summer.

There are frequent rail and bus services linking the ports with London and other cities and towns.

● Information and reservations can be obtained from most travel agents or directly from the ferry companies: **Brittany Ferries,** The Brittany Centre, Wharf Road, Portsmouth, Hampshire PO2 8RU (☎ 0705 827701) (Plymouth/Roscoff, St. Malo, Santander).

Information

● **Sealink British Ferries,** PO Box 29, London SW1V 1JX (☎ 01-834 8122) (Folkestone/Boulogne, Dover/Calais, Portsmouth/Cherbourg, Weymouth/Cherbourg, Harwich/Hook of Holland) (inquiries and reservations in most major British Rail booking offices).

● **P. and O.,** Enterprise House, Channel View Road, Dover, Kent CT17 9TJ (☎ 0304 203388) (Dover/Zeebrugge, Felixstowe/Zeebrugge, Dover/Boulogne, Dover/Calais, Portsmouth/Cherbourg, Portsmouth/Le Havre).

● **Hoverspeed UK Ltd,** Maybrook House, Queens Gardens, Dover CT17 9UQ (☎ 0304 240241 and 02 554 7061) (Dover/Ostend, Dover/Calais).

● **DFDS Seaways,** Parkeston Quay, Harwich, Essex CO12 4SY (☎ 0255 508933) (Harwich/Esjberg, Esjberg/Newcastle, Harwich/Hamburg, Harwich/Gothenburg, Newcastle/Gothenburg).

● **Fred Olsen Lines,** Victoria Plaza 111 Buckingham Palace Road, London SW1W OSP (☎ 01-630 0033) (Harwich/Kristiansand, Harwich/Oslo, Hirthals/Harwich).

● **Sally Line,** 81 Piccadilly, London W1 (☎ 01-409 2240) (Ramsgate/Dunkirk).

Britain is linked into Europe's extensive, fast rail system which links with main passenger ferry services across the Channel and hence to London. Reduced fares are available for students and senior citizens.

Rail

BR Inter City Europe passenger information: ☎ 01-834 2345. All calls are answered in strict rotation (→section on rail travel).

Customs, passports and visas

Entry requirements for Britain vary according to the nationality of the visitor and the length and purpose of the trip. On arrival you must produce a valid national passport or other document satisfactorily establishing your identity and nationality. You do not need a visa if you are a citizen of the Commonwealth (including Australia, Canada and New Zealand), the Republic of South Africa or the USA. If you are not a citizen of an EEC country, you may be asked to com-

Passports and visas

plete a landing card before you pass through passport control. The immigration officer will place an endorsement in your passport that will probably impose a time limit on your stay. Other conditions may restrict your freedom to take employment or require you to register with the police.

Information

Should you wish to extend your stay or seek a variation of any conditions attached to it, write, before the expiry date of your permitted stay, to the Under Secretary of State, Home Office, Immigration Department, Lunar House, Wellesley Road, Croydon CR9 2BY, Surrey (☎ 01-686 0688), enclosing your passport or national identity card and form IS120 if these were your entry documents.

Customs

A colour-coded customs method is employed at most ports and airports in Britain. Go through the Red Channel if you have goods to declare (or if you are unsure of importation restrictions), or the Green Channel (which is subject to spot-checks by a customs officer) if you have nothing to declare. Visitors arriving in cars can obtain red or green windscreen (windshield) stickers on the boat. Where this system is not in operation, report to the customs officer in the baggage hall.

Visitors to Britain may leave with limited amounts of alcoholic drink, tobacco, perfumes and gifts free of import duty. Visitors from EEC countries are subject to two distinct allowance rates: (a) for goods obtained duty and tax free in the EEC, or duty and tax free on a ship or an aircraft, or goods obtained outside the EEC and (b) for goods obtained duty and tax paid within the EEC. Details of these allowances are available at most ports of entry to Britain.

Restrictions are enforced regarding importation of certain specialized goods, including controlled drugs; firearms; fireworks and ammunition; counterfeit coins; meat and poultry and most of their products (cooked or uncooked), including eggs and milk; animals and birds. Licenses can be granted for the importation of firearms, animals and birds.

Goods requiring a license for export include the following: controlled drugs, firearms and ammunition, most animals and birds and certain goods derived from protected species (e.g., furskins and ivory). You must declare anything you intend to leave or sell in Britain.

VAT

Tax relief: In Britain, except in the Channel Islands, Value Added Tax (VAT) is charged on most goods at a standard rate of 15 percent (at time of going to press). It is also charged at the standard rate on services you may receive, for example in hotels, restaurants and on car rental. VAT on services may not be reclaimed, but visitors can take advantage of the *Retail Export Scheme*, whereby they can reclaim VAT on goods purchased for export. *NB:* Not all shops operate the scheme, and there is often a minimum purchase price, as well as minimum values which apply to travelers from EEC countries. Shops operating the scheme will ask to see your passport before completing the VAT form. This form must be presented, with the goods, to the customs office at the point of departure from Britain (or to customs at the point of importation into an EEC country if you qualify as a Community traveler), within three months of purchase. After the customs officer has certified the form it should be returned to the shopkeeper, who will then send you the VAT refund, from which a small administration fee may be deducted.

English Customs Information Centre: HM Customs and Excise, Dorset House, Stamford Street, London SE1 9PS (☎ 01-928 0533).

British Tourist Authority (BTA)

BTA

Tourism is now Britain's biggest growth industry. The **British Tourist Authority**, represented in many cities abroad, is the single source of information on all aspects of Britain for the traveler preparing a visit.

In addition to promoting tourism to Britain from overseas, the BTA's responsibilities are to advise the government on tourism matters affecting Britain as a whole and to encourage the provision and improvement of tourist amenities and facilities in Britain.

Located at Thames Tower, Black's Road, London W6 9EL (☎ 01-846 9000), the BTA works in close cooperation with the four **National Tourist Boards** — England, Scotland, Wales and Northern Ireland — as well as with the **Regional Tourist Boards, local government authorities** and other principal **tourism organizations**.

Tourism organizations

The BTA's overseas offices work closely with all tourist interests in the territories for which they are responsible, including leading travel agents and tour operators. The overseas offices are provided with a wide range of professional, technical and creative services by BTA staff in London. Services offered abroad include the distribution of numerous free leaflets and information on a wide range of subjects including suggested travel itineraries, methods of travel, useful addresses, accommodation, tourist attractions and events.

Information

● **British Tourist Authority offices abroad:**

Australia and New Zealand: Associated Midland House, 171 Clarence Street, Sydney, NSW 2000 (☎ 010 61 2 29 8627).

Belgium and Luxembourg: 52 Rue de la Montagne/Bergstraat, Brussels 1000 (☎ 010 32 2 511 43 90).

Canada: Suite 600, 94 Cumberland Street, Toronto, Ont. M5R 3N3 (☎ 010 1 416 961 8124/925 6326).

Denmark: Montergade 3, 1116 Copenhagen K (☎ 010 45 1 12 07 93).

France: 65 rue Pierre Charron, 75008 Paris (☎ 010 42 89 11 11).

West Germany: 6000 Frankfurt 1, Neue Mainzer Strasse 22 (☎ 010 49 69 23 8075011).

Holland: Aurora Gebouw 5E, Stadhouderskade 2, 1054 ES Amsterdam (☎ 010 91 85 50 51).

Italy: Via S. Eufemia 5, 00187 Rome (☎ 010 39 6 678 55 48).

Japan: 246 Tokyo Club Building, 3-2-6 Kasumigaseki, Chiyoda-ku, Tokyo 100 (☎ 010 81 3 581 3603).

Mexico: Edificio Alber, Paseo de la Reforma 332-5, Piso 06600 Mexico DF (☎ 010 525 533 6375).

Norway: Fridtiof Nansens Plass, 0160 Oslo 1 (☎ 010 47 2 41 18 49).

Singapore: 14 Collyer Quay 05-03, Singapore Rubber House, Singapore 0104 (☎ 010 65 2242966/7).

Spain and Portugal: Torre de Madrid 6/4, Plaza de Espana, 28008 Madrid (☎ 010 34 1 241 13 96).

Sweden and Finland: Malmskillnadsgatan 42, Box 7293, s -103 90 Stockholm 40 (☎ 010 46 8 21 24 44).

Switzerland: Limmatquai 78, 8001 Zurich (☎ 010 41 1 47 42 77/97).

USA: 3rd floor, 40 West 57th Street, New York NY 10019 (☎ 010 1 212 581 4700); 350 S. Figueroa Street, Los Angeles, California 90017 (☎ 010 1 213 628 3525); John Hancock Centre, 875 North Michigan Avenue, Chicago Ill 60611 (☎ 010 1 312 787 0490); Cedar Marple Plaza, Suite 2305, Cedar Springs Road, Lock Box 346, Dallas, Texas 75201 (☎ 010 1 214 720 4040).

● **National Tourist Offices:**

English Tourist Board, Thames Tower, Black's Road, Hammersmith, London W6 9EL (☎ 01-846 9000).

Scottish Tourist Board, 23 Ravelston Terrace, Edinburgh EH4 3EU (☎ 031-332 2433).

Welsh Tourist Board, Brunel House, 2 Fitzalan Road, Cardiff CF2 1UY (☎ 0222-499909).

Northern Ireland Tourist Board, River House, 48 High Street, Belfast BT1 2DS (☎ 0232 231221).

● **Regional Tourist Boards:**

The Regional Tourist Boards are subdivided into 'local' **tourist information centres** (TICs) which can provide detailed and often 'off-beat' information about the town or village in which they are situated. There are more than 700 throughout Great Britain (addresses: individual town sections). Most TICs are in town centres, often in places such as a historic building, a library or a specially designed trailer, and signposted throughout the town by an 'ic'. Staff should be able to answer any queries regarding local attractions and can supply written details of local events. Many centres will make an accommodation reservation for the same night in their locality (at a marginal cost) and several centres operate the *Book-a-Bed-Ahead Service* (BABA) which can, for a small fee, make a reservation for accommodation in any other town that also operates the service, for the same or next night.

● **The London Tourist Information Centre** (serving the Greater London Area) is on the forecourt of Victoria Station, London SW1, with a telephone information service on 01-730 3488, Mon. to Fri., 9am-5:30 pm (automatic system — hold until a receptionist answers). Written inquiries to: **LVCB,** Central Information Unit, 26 Grosvenor Gardens, London SW1W ODU.

● **British Travel Centre,** Rex House, 4-12 Lower Regent Street, London SW1 (☎ 01-730 3400). Telephone service is open Mon. to Fri., 9am-6:30pm; Sat., 10am-5pm; closed Sun. The centre is open Mon. to Fri., 9am-6:30pm; Sat., 10am-6pm and Sun., 10am-4pm for tourist information and leaflets, on air, rail, bus and car travel; sightseeing tours; accommodation; theatre seats; money exchange; gift and book shops; and displays of forthcoming attractions in Britain.

Money

You may bring in sterling notes, foreign currency notes, travelers' checks, letter of credit, etc. in any currency and up to any amount. There is no restriction on the value of travelers' checks you can change. The British money system is based on decimalization. There are one hundred **pence** to each **pound** sterling. Notes are issued to the value of £50, £20, £10 and £5. Coins are issued to the value of £1, 50p, 20p, 10p, 5p, 2p, and 1p. In Scotland, Northern Ireland, the Channel Islands and the Isle of Man, local bank notes are widely used, as well as the national bank notes. These are different in design and colour, but are of exactly the same value. If necessary, you can exchange them for normal Bank of England notes at any bank in England and Wales. There is no handling charge.

Banks

You will get the best rate of exchange at any branch of the main British clearing banks: Barclays, Lloyds, Midland and National Westminster. Banks are open Mon. to Fri. from 9:30am to 3:30pm, except Scotland where they close for one hour at lunchtime. At weekends and on public holidays you can go to one of the money exchanges at the airports or in central London and other major cities, or you can change travelers' checks at big travel agents such as Thomas Cook (they have more than 200 offices throughout the country) or at the larger hotels and some department stores. Non-bank commission charges vary considerably.

Information

Barclays, 54 Lombard Street, London EC3P 3AH (☎ 01-283 2161); Lloyds, 71 Lombard Street, London EC3 (☎ 01-626 1500); Midland, Poultry, London EC2 (☎ 01-606 9911); National Westminster, 41 Lothbury, London EC2P 2BP (☎ 01-726 1000).

Major exchange offices

London: Eurochange Bureaux Ltd (open 7 days a week), 95 Buckingham Palace Road, London SW1 (☎ 01-828 4953); offices at the following underground stations: Knightsbridge, Gloucester Road, Tottenham Court Road, Kings Cross and Embankment; Deak International (open 7 days a week), 22 Leinster Terrace, London W2 (☎ 01-402 5128); offices at 15 Shaftesbury Avenue, London W1; 237 Oxford Street, London W1; 2 London Street, Paddington W2; 2 Pembridge Road, London W2; and in Kings Cross and Liverpool Street stations; Thomas Cook Head Office, 45 Berkeley Street, London W1 (☎ 01-499 4000); Heathrow Airport: Barclays and Midland Banks (open 7 days a week, one 24 hours); Gatwick Airport: Lloyds and Midland Banks (open 24 hours, 7 days a week); Glasgow Airport: Clydesdale Bank (open 7 days a week).

Credit cards

The Visa card is by far the most widely accepted credit card in Britain.

Diners Club, Access/Eurocard/Mastercharge and American Express cards are less widely accepted, although these organizations do have very extensive British networks. (The American Express organization, 6 Haymarket, London SW1 (☎ 01-930 4411) also provides a wide range of banking, credit card, travel and other services for visitors.)

★ In case of loss: Visa: (☎ 0604 21288); American Express: (☎ 0273 696933/01-551 1111); Diners Club: (☎ 0252 516261); Access/Eurocard/Mastercharge: (☎ 01-636 7878).

Emergencies

Medical

If a traveler becomes ill in Britain, or if an existing condition worsens to the extent that treatment cannot be delayed until he or she returns home, he or she is entitled to free *National Health Service* (NHS) treatment including treatment at NHS Accident and Emergency departments of hospitals. Emergency dental treatment can be obtained in the same way. If, however, it is necessary to stay overnight or longer in a hospital, you will probably be asked to pay. You are therefore strongly advised to take out adequate insurance coverage before traveling to Britain (consult your broker or travel agent for a suitable policy). The telephone operator (dial 100) will give you the telephone number and address of the local NHS doctor's surgery, or you can go to the casualty department of any general hospital.

In cases of emergency, dial 999 (the free nationwide emergency number) and ask for either 'Fire', 'Police' or 'Ambulance'. State that you are a foreign tourist, the nature of your problem and your location.

Pharmacies

In every town or city district at least one pharmacy remains open for one hour on Sundays and public holidays. The local police station will have a list of pharmacies providing this service. London: 50 Willesden Lane, NW6 (☎ 01-624 8000) (24 hours daily).

Post and telephone

Post

The postal system in Britain is run by the state-controlled *Post Office*, while the telephone system is now owned and run by a private organization, *British Telecom*.

Post offices, generally, are open from 9am-5:30pm from Mon. to Fri.,

9am-12:30pm on Sat., although smaller town and village offices sometimes close for lunch. Stamps can normally only be bought at post offices although they can sometimes be bought from a machine outside larger branches. There are no collections on Sundays and the final weekend collection is usually about midday on Saturdays. The largest post office, **open 24 hours daily,** is in St. Martin's-le-Grand, London EC1 (☎ 01-432 1234). Telephone directories from all over the world can be consulted there. The main post office in each city or town handles **poste restante** and letters can be collected (for a small fee) upon production of proof of identity.

Telephone

Most public telephone booths are now made of smoked glass and have the yellow British Telecom insignia (though the old telephone boxes survive in some areas). Many public buildings, post offices, pubs and shops have payphones inside. There are three types of payphone: 1) dial coinbox, operated by 5p and 10p coins; 2) push-button coinbox, suitable for calls to most places in Western Europe and a few other countries, which accept 2p, 10p and 50p coins (minimum 6p); 3) cardphones, becoming more widely available. Cardphones are clearly marked — to use them you must buy a special card available from post offices and certain shops near cardphones. You may then make any number of calls in a cardphone up to the value of the card, without needing cash.

Telephone rates

National charges: Different types of calls cost different amounts, depending on when and to where you make them. There are three call rates that relate to different times of the day and week: peak rate is between 9am-1pm, Mon. to Fri.; standard rate is between 8am-9am and between 1pm-6pm, Mon. to Fri.; cheap rate is between 6pm-8am, Mon. to Fri. and all day and night at weekends.

International Direct Dialing (IDD) charges: Direct dialing is possible to anywhere within Great Britain and to most countries overseas if dialing from London. There are a lot of digits involved once you start dialing overseas, but by avoiding operator-assisted calls, costs are cut considerably and rates are reasonable. On IDD calls you pay only for the length of time you are connected. The cost of an IDD call varies depending on which Charge Band the country you are calling is in and the time of day. An IDD cheap rate is available to most countries, which differs in time from national call rates. Avoid calls through hotel switchboards — as much as 300-400 percent of the phone charge can be added to the bill by the individual hotel.

There are three types of dialing code — local, national and international. **Codes** Local codes apply to your local call area (details are in the British Telecom code book supplied with all private and public telephones). All areas, down to the smallest village, have their own national (STD) code which is fixed. It usually begins with the number 0 and must always be dialed at the beginning of a call from virtually anywhere in the UK, and from overseas minus the 0. In certain cases, local area codes may apply for calls to nearby exchanges.

Attended call bureaus: These are located in a very few main post offices. The caller pays in advance and an attendant connects the call. Charges are by the minute. New style bureaus can be found in a few places where you dial your own call to any of over 100 countries throughout the world and pay only for the time you have used. Central London Bureau: 1 Broadway, Victoria, London SW1, plus in Oxford, Cambridge, London Heathrow and Gatwick airports and (during the summer) in Chester, Perth and Fort William, Scotland.

Free calls: The most important, in addition to the emergency 999 numbers, is the operator (dial 100). For free directory inquiries, dial 142 for a London number and 192 for numbers outside London. International directory inquiry numbers are listed in the BT code book under the names of the individual countries.

Museums and art galleries

Britain is home to a vast collection of works of art from all over the world. Although some small percentage of this remains in private hands, the better portion is on display in the nation's great museums, not to mention hundreds of country houses that are as notable for the collections housed within as for their often stunning architecture. (For example, England's **National Portrait Gallery** maintains two collections outside London at **Montacute**, Somerset and at **Beningbrough**, North Yorkshire.) Britain's museums are usually well designed, with good lighting. Despite recent cutbacks in government support of the arts, admission to most museums and art galleries is free (although a charge may be made for specialist collections and exhibitions, and a few ask for a voluntary donation) and they are open every day except on principal holidays. London's national museums and galleries contain some of the richest treasures in the world and offer a service of advice and scholarly reference. The **British Museum**, the **Victoria and Albert Museum** and other national museums give expert opinion on the age or identity of objects or paintings, but will not give a valuation. Lecture programs are usually offered as well. Most museums and galleries have a shop near the entrance selling pamphlets and booklets on the various collections, postcards, posters and general souvenirs.

Details of exhibitions

Check the daily events listings in local newspapers and tourist information centres. In London, *Time Out* and *City Limits* magazines are the most comprehensive. See *The Shell Guide to Small Country Museums* and *The Good Museum Guide*, both by Kenneth Hudson.

The locations of Britain's principal museums are shown on the map and details can be found in the gazetteer section entries.